NORTHEASTERN
WILDS

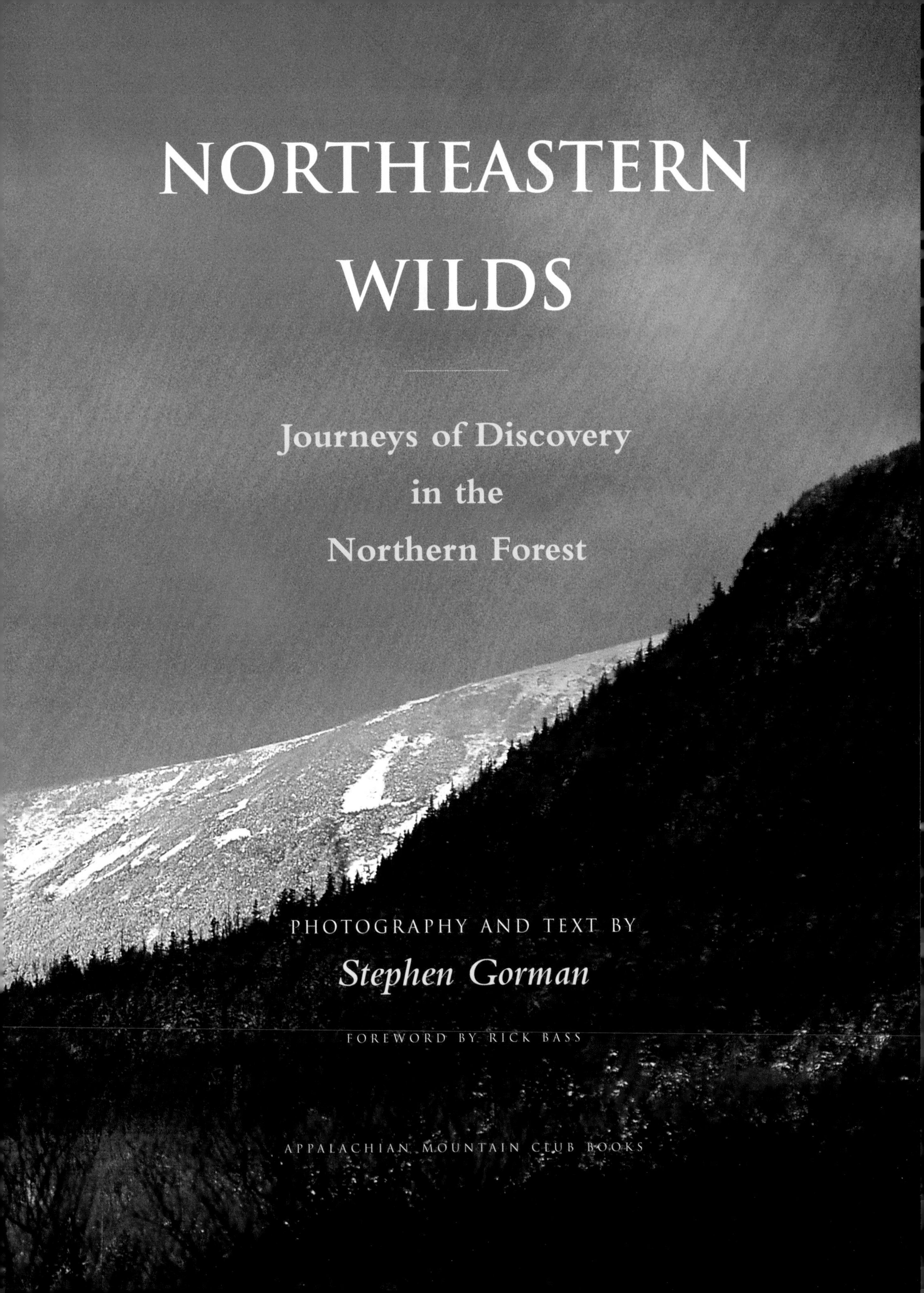

NORTHEASTERN WILDS

Journeys of Discovery
in the
Northern Forest

PHOTOGRAPHY AND TEXT BY

Stephen Gorman

FOREWORD BY RICK BASS

APPALACHIAN MOUNTAIN CLUB BOOKS

DEDICATED TO THE MEMORY OF
MARTIN LEIGHTON, MAINE WOODSMAN

DESIGN BY DEDE CUMMINGS DESIGNS

Library of Congress Cataloging-in-Publication Data
Gorman, Stephen.
Northeastern wilds : journeys of discovery in the northern forest;
photography and text by Stephen Gorman ; foreword by Rick Bass.
    p. cm.
ISBN 1-929173-09-1 (hard cover : alk. paper)
1. Forests and forestry—New England. 2. Forest conservation
—New England.   I. Title.
  QH104.5.N4G67 2002
  508.74--dc21   2002009657

Printed in Canada

COVER: *Alpenglow on Barren Ledge overlooking Onawa Lake, Appalachian Trail, Maine.*
INSET HALF-TITLE PAGE: *Au Sable River, Adirondack Park, New York.*
TITLE PAGE DOUBLE-SPREAD: *Gulf of Slides, Presidential Range, New Hampshire.*
OPPOSITE PAGE: *A ribbon of water pours through a rocky cleft in the White Mountains, New Hampshire.*

CONTENTS

FOREWORD

S UDDENLY, we're not the same nation. There is in almost all of us a place, even if some days only a small place—a postage-stamp-sized place—that is off-balance, frightened, pensive, even confused. And only now are we beginning to accept some of the basic truths about this small world, truths that we have previously been denying or debating for decades: that species extinction is rampant, perhaps unstoppable; that clear-cuts are crazed expressions of raw madness; that global warming is a reality, and that the mass of our numbers, and our consumptions, are accelerating it; and that the heart of man is unchanging, always capable of great evil as well as great love.

Against such hard and ancient truths, and the breathless force of their disclosure in this century which, like all the ones before it, is too often a century of war, I take increasing solace in the logic, grace, and unimpeachable democracy of those wildernesses that still remain intact, and particularly our last native wildernesses, as opposed to those of distant lands, or the now-mythical wildernesses of storybooks. I think we are all, even if we had not previously given much thought to such things, reconsidering the beauty of the green force, the wilderness icon, as a core or essence of some deeper meaning and order, and a force more enduring than even our own most magnificent artifices of city and stone.

The Swift River tumbles out of New Hampshire's White Mountains on a flawless autumn day.

In the midst of such reemerging understanding, the goals of those who propose to protect the East's greatest treasure—the Northern Forest, and our other last remaining wildlands—seem to me to be long overdue—a punctuation mark on the dream of Henry Thoreau, 150 years earlier—and one of the most patriotic place-based solutions to the challenge of the times that I can imagine.

The Northern Forest consists of twenty-six million acres of wildland—some public, but much private, its fate hanging in the balance: Wilderness or strip malls? Forests or subdivisions? Reaching across New York's Adirondack Park, Vermont, New Hampshire, and into Maine, the Northern Forest is far and away the largest remaining wild forest in the East—though it's in danger of being skinned alive and swallowed hole. In the last three years alone, more than 6 million acres of forest land have been auctioned off by the timber companies-turned-real-estate-speculators, who perform this reverse alchemy, turning gold into mire.

For all the drama of the goal of restoring and protecting the Northern Forest—the largest and most commonsense, forward-looking vision this country has had since the long-ago dream of creating the first National Park at Yellowstone—even this dream remains moderate. Such has been, and remains, our appetite for the world, however, that it's simply one of the best dreams we have remaining: a grand opportunity to express reverence for, and to celebrate, one of our country's last intact pieces of original landscape, original creation.

All over the Northeast, and all over the country, such dreams—some large, some small—are metamorphosing into action. Local land trusts are being established, and conservation easements drafted as we increasingly begin to consider what legacy we will leave to our children and their generation. Wanting, in an imperfect world, to leave them some example of perfect beauty.

Incredible conservation initiatives, particularly in the Northeast, are being implemented: 500,000 acres here, 600,000 acres there. Often I feel that we in the West are a hundred years behind the times. And conversely, I find myself too often devoting six months to fighting for a 10-acre logging unit; two or three years, defending, and then trying to mitigate, a 100-acre parcel. This is no way to live a life as either an activist or a "regular" person, but I sometimes justify such wretched battles by taking solace in staring, late at night, at the last and larger blank spots on the map, in the last few such places where they can still be found. The solace of these larger dreams is what provides success and fuel for such maddening little battles.

In every generation of man, I suspect, there has always been the fear, the lament, that time is accelerating—and that with each day, the freedoms of a life and a culture, freedoms that have gone relatively unquestioned for the last many generations, are vanishing fast now, along with so many other things: icebergs, grizzly bears, clean air and water, open space, wild forests—all once birthrights, and yet all now in dire threat of disappearing within even our own short lives.

"Of what avail are forty freedoms," wrote Aldo Leopold, "without a blank spot on the map?"

In such a time of perhaps unprecedented impermanence, it is these last blank spots on the map that the eye often turns toward, dreaming of integrity, wholeness, and restoration; of the absence of fragmentation. In wild places, wild forests, however—unlike the human heart, which is still so often confused or uncertain or hesitant—abstractions such as integrity are made startlingly, specifically, beautifully real. Steve Gorman's photographs come as close as is possible, other than actually being in the woods, to giving us the glimpses, tastes, odors, sounds, and touches of the spirit and being of these places.

These are not small pictures in this book. Somehow, they depict space and time, though the words we might use to describe them, in our puniness, might be their opposites—spaciousness and timelessness. So it seems to us. And so, in our perceptions, they become. And too often, we, as a culture, then treat these vast lands, these "howling wildernesses," as if they are unbounded.

Gorman's text explains what many of the photographs do not: that although there is in all of wild nature a seed or essence of immediacy, so too is there in the heart of man the magnificent yet puzzling power—the ability, if you will—to take away this essence, to exterminate entire species, entire ecosystems. That our own force, our own consumptions, have become geological in their immensity, and that, quite simply put, we're using up what little wilderness we have left.

Not all of the photographs, of course, portray time and its immensity, and wild landscape—the glorious pigments on the canvas of time. Some of the most breathtaking pictures show the taking-away, and the illness, rather than the giving-back, and the preserving. Any one drunk on the ambrosia of often-imaginary individual "rights," while shunning almost completely the associated and more mature elixir of "responsibilities," need only look at a single photo of the clear-cuts overtaking the Northern Forest (as they continue to overtake the last of the West), to begin to consider, perhaps for the first time, the far more destructive, freedom-robbing foreclosure of opportunity left in the wake of such mindless industrial greed—the greed, the American plague, of never-coming-back. The plague of placelessness.

Gorman intelligently explores the seemingly unnatural alliances and collaborations that are beginning to arise in an effort to preserve the Northern Forest—hunters and anglers and hikers sitting down with independent lumbermen (those few who still remain), as well as the budget-harried local county

commissioners and school clerks and chambers-of-commerce, as they begin to do the hard work of mapping out longer-term visions whose arc will, for once, perhaps, extend further than the next quarterly earnings statement. Plans such as the Northern Forest, whose arc, hopefully, will cover the next 150 years with rest, healing, and preservation as much a component of this forward-arc as voraciousness, short-sightedness, and aggressive squandering has been a component of the back-arc.

A magnificent sugar maple displays its autumn colors in New Hampshire's White Mountains.

In this, too, the East, and the progress of the Northern Forest, can be a model for the West, and the rest of the country, as we come up hard, finally, and for only the first time, against the limits of space and time—the end of the timber and mining frontier, and of subsidized corporate high-grading; the end, finally, of the Big Rock Candy Mountain. This books shows us this dream.

Even the most elegant dream, however, is of little use, eventually, without action. Dreams wither and die, unacted upon, and drain back down into the soil they escaped from, sometimes for centuries at a time, other times never reemerging.

As the history of our country has shown, our blank spots do not tend to remain blank for very long. Register others to vote, write letters, join alliances,

send in dues, talk to neighbors, friends and family about this dream, and dream larger, and work harder, please, in the name of securing what remains of a wild and hopefully enduring national homeland. The U.S. Congress and administration, as well, needs to hear from you loud and clear, with insistent dignity on our part, about the utterly clamant need to protect the last of our American wilderness—a domestic problem that has been languishing unresolved for decades, even centuries, almost always shoved to the back of the line behind other more urgent, pressing matters. Against the near-geologic scale of a wild forest, nearly every other concern of mankind will almost always seem to be more immediate and pressing.

In the meantime, our wilderness is slipping away, being clear-cut and bladed and mined and dammed, dissolving to dream, to memory, then to nothing.

All of a sudden, it's past time to protect it. It's not too late, but it's past time. A hundred and fifty years is long enough for any dream to germinate, grow, and prosper. Enough political gridlock, enough clear-cutting, enough loss. Preserve the Northern Forest.

RICK BASS

THE LOST NATION

✦

WEST OF QUODDY HEAD, east of Lake Ontario, and south of the Saint
Lawrence River lies a land Henry David Thoreau called "a damp and
intricate wilderness . . . even more grim and wild than you had anticipated." So
it was in Thoreau's day, and so much of it remains: a swath of forest and mountains and lakes that seems to stretch beyond the rim of the world.

This is not an official geographic region—precisely designated, bound
and mapped—so much as a land traced by the wanderings of moose, the flight
of migrating geese, and the haunting call of the common loon. It is a largely
untamed land of rockbound coasts, dark forests, rushing rivers, and alpine summits. It's also a place rich in human history, the ancestral home of the Abenaki
and the object of French and English dreams of empire.

But in many ways this land we call the Northern Forest is a place apart, a
secret, private realm bypassed and mostly forgotten by mainstream society. It's
a place where there really is a secluded mountain valley named Lost Nation, a
bit of poetry of place that captures the essence of the entire region.

The Northern Forest is a place of stunning beauty and startling drama. In
the Saranac Lakes, green islands sail on cool breezes flowing from high rocky
summits. Verdant chasms guard secret pools beneath the leafy slopes of the
Green Mountains. The piercing winter wind on Lake Umbagog can blow you
off your feet and blind you with a wall of swirling snow. The northern lights

*Majestic trees
reach for the
sky in the
Northern
Forest.*

OVERLEAF:
*Attean Pond,
Maine, at
sunset.*

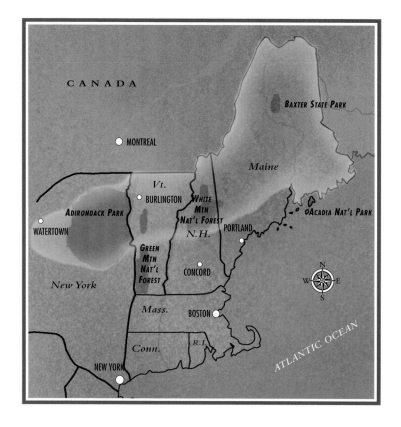

dance above the spruce on clear nights near Chesuncook while coyotes raise their wavering harmonies to the stars.

There was a time when the power of this land intimidated those who ventured here. The Puritans feared the dark forest, calling it "a howling wilderness, where none inhabited but hellish fiends, and brutish men that devil's [sic] worshipped."

This land was somewhat less fearsome to Thoreau, who found that, "generally speaking, a howling wilderness does not howl," but even he ventured forth with some trepidation. "Nature was here something savage and awful, though beautiful," he wrote. At one point on Maine's Mount Katahdin the power of untamed nature overcame him, causing him to question his very being.

Native Americans thrived in the Northern Forest, following a seasonal migration from the forest to the sea, taking full advantage of what the land and waters had to offer. Whether through limited technology, a heightened sense of stewardship, or a combination of both, Native Americans left few permanent scars upon the landscape. And so, after some ten thousand years of unbroken human occupation, Thoreau could still look around and claim that here was "the fresh and natural surface of the planet Earth, as it was made forever and ever."

Later visitors did make their mark in the Northern Forest, leaving baffling place-names on the map that offer tantalizing clues to an intriguing past. What happened at Pond of Safety, Misery Knob, and Blood Cove? Who knows the story of Ghost Landing Bar, Fool Killer Mountain, and Smuggler's Cave? Some of the riddles left behind are scattered in obscure or hidden locations. Where, for example, is the Dead Diamond River? Does anyone know Unknown

OPPOSITE:
Mount Chocorua rising above Chocorua Lake, New Hampshire.

OVERLEAF:
Hidden streams flow through a Green Mountain forest in peak foliage, Vermont.

Pond? Who has climbed a summit called Fat Mans Woe, or run a canoe through Kill-Me-Quick Rapids?

Sometimes the story behind the name survives. On the East Branch of the Penobscot River there is a rapid called The Hulling Machine. This frothy, snaggletooth cataract was named by the Bangor Tigers, those rough-and-tumble woodchoppers and river drivers who wrestled the long logs down the icy, turbulent East Branch to the mills in Bangor. When those magnificent white pines emerged from The Hulling Machine, they came out gleaming: all of the bark had been stripped off by the rocks.

Today, much as it was when Thoreau passed through, the Northern Forest is a place where we can experience the power and indifference of wild nature. Confronted by the immensity of empty space, we feel awed, diminished, and insignificant. There, as in a great cathedral or holy shrine, lives something bigger and more powerful than we are. At these times we gain a perspective that is ordinarily denied us.

This power, this mystery—the same that confronted Thoreau—is still present. I know because I have felt it, although I really didn't expect to. Early on I dismissed my home region as too developed and overcrowded. I knew this had been the frontier at one time, but that was long ago, back in the days when Roger's Rangers skulked through the North Woods looking for French soldiers to bury their hatchets in. Now, the place was too tame, I thought. And so, like many other young people seeking wide open spaces and adventure, I headed west.

Between surveying claims in Alaska's Brooks Range, wrangling horses in Wyoming, and attending classes in Colorado, I returned home for visits. Each time I explored a little more of the region and began to compare what I saw with what was happening to the West.

A rain-swollen stream flows through a gap in the Green Mountains, Vermont.

The West of my imagination was disappearing fast. Between the strip mines, pipelines, oil fields, clear-cuts, irrigation projects, highway construction, and especially the sprawling new cities gobbling up open space, a map of the West looked like a coach's chalkboard at halftime. In Colorado, where I lived, wooden surveyor stakes flying orange flagging tape marched like an invading army across the plains and up into the canyons, marking out new cul-de-sacs, fast-food emporiums, and car dealerships. Wistfully, I thought of mountain men Kit Carson and Old Bill Williams, of Plains Indians Black Kettle and White Antelope—of those who had seen the land when it was new—and I decided it was time to head home for a while.

One day, with the Colorado Rockies in the rearview mirror, I headed

across the sere brown Cheyenne and Arapaho grasslands toward the rising sun.
I made it my mission to explore my own backyard, to get to know the place I
now embraced as home ground.

Years after climbing nameless peaks in the Arctic, I finally stood atop
Katahdin's Knife Edge in Maine on a crisp February day. After rafting the Snake,
I finally paddled the Raquette. After hiking through giant Douglas fir groves on
the Olympic Peninsula, I finally picked my way through a tangle of blown-
down balsam fir somewhere in the middle of the Northern Forest.

On those trips I discovered a wild realm as vast as anything I'd seen out
West. But when I told my friends about what I had seen and experienced,
most of them—even lifelong Yankees—had never heard of the places I was

A blazing
autumn
mountainside
in the
Adirondacks,
New York.

11

describing. And when I mentioned that a mere few hours' drive north of Boston timber wolves might well be repopulating a forest so huge, so lost, that during the Cold War the U.S. Air Force used it to practice bombing runs because of its resemblance to Siberia, they looked at me as though I were demented.

But the facts were undeniable. I got people's attention when I pointed out that New York's Adirondack Park is the largest park of any kind in the lower forty-eight states. At more than six million acres, or ten thousand square miles, the Adirondack Park is larger than Massachusetts and twice as large as Yellowstone and Yosemite National Parks combined. A natural treasure chest, the Adirondack Park is a United Nations International Biosphere Reserve. And when I mentioned that the largest uninhabited region in the lower forty-eight states was not in the sagebrush deserts of Wyoming or Nevada but in the northern forests of Maine, my listeners were invariably shocked. How could a state that was home to the country's first chartered town—York, in 1642—have remained so wild for three and a half centuries?

On many of those journeys through the region I discovered an uncompromising Old Testament kind of place, a harsh and unforgiving land where life goes on much as it used to, where nature is still in charge. Far from malls, freeways, and suburbs, I found an America that seemed to be on the verge of disappearing altogether.

Voices in the Forest

We never ceded this land. Our lands stretch from southern Quebec to western Maine and all the way to northern Massachusetts. We lost it to gun-barrel diplomacy. 🌲

CHIEF HOMER ST. FRANCIS, *Abenaki activist and direct descendent of Chief Gray Lock.*

There were places in the Northern Forest where I felt a timelessness I know can only be experienced in the wildest places. In the autumn woods, gray, scuddy clouds threatened snow. Swirling wind lifted the flaming leaves from maples, birch, and poplar. Out on the big lakes the water was a cold gun-barrel blue. Whitecaps with deep troughs rolled on past uninhabited shores. There was a remarkable sense that nothing had changed, that everything was as it should be.

Touring the woods and waters alone, with friends, and in the company of guides, writers, environmentalists, hunters, woods workers, foresters, recreationalists, and developers, I learned that the forests and mountains of northern New England and New York boast some of the most arresting natural beauty on the planet.

Here was a rugged landscape of thick boreal forests, blazing autumn hillsides, snowy granite peaks, and vast wilderness lakes. Here were the headwaters of mighty rivers, including the Hudson, the Connecticut, the Androscoggin, the Kennebec, the Penobscot, and the St. John. Here too were mountains, forests, and wetlands meeting the cold North Atlantic, northern and temperate climate zones overlapping, and a profusion of terrestrial, aquatic, and avian life flourishing.

But I also found that unlike the West, where immense public landholdings are managed by federal and state agencies to accommodate visitors from across the country and around the world, just a small percentage of the wildlands in the Northern Forest are permanently protected by public ownership. It is to these few holdings that most visitors travel, not knowing that many of the area's natural treasures lie far off the popular tourist routes. Many of these gems remain hidden because they are part of a private domain owned by outside interests for whom the land is often a mere abstraction, an item on a balance sheet. I learned, for example, that of the 26-million acres in the Northern Forest, less than 20 percent is publicly owned. A whopping 85 percent of Maine is privately owned by multinational paper corporations. (Just 4 percent of Maine is in public ownership, whereas in Utah, for example, the public owns 65 percent of the land.)

A red maple leaf rests on meadow grass wet with morning dew in New Hampshire.

A stump in a clear-cut near Moosehead Lake, Maine.

And the more I traveled, the more I saw, the more I realized that much of the Northern Forest is in pretty rough shape, for while the landscape is vast and unpopulated much of it is covered with stumps. I flew in bush planes over 60-square-mile clear-cuts in Maine, a state carved up by more than 20,000 miles of logging roads—the largest private road system in the world. At times all I could see from that aerial platform was a wasteland of stumps, skidder ruts, and slash windrows.

Rather than acting as proof of the eternal or a bulwark against change, these sites caused me to despair—the wild character of the forest seemed beyond salvage, for it appeared to have been liquidated. As an ancient World War I veteran who lived on the shores of Grand Lake Matagamon told me, "In the old days the logging companies were more selective. Now they come in and take everything. I don't understand it."

I came away from these trips feeling that the Northern Forest is both a realm of unsurpassed natural beauty and a plundered province whose fortune has been ripped out to enrich corporations based not in Millinocket, Berlin, Island Pond, and Watertown but in places like Stamford, Johannesburg, Tokyo, and Richmond.

Though the practices of corporate forestry can be devastating, the consequences of large-scale land transfers to private developers may be even worse. Both the foresters and environmentalists I traveled with agreed that a clear-cut, no matter how huge, is still open space—something will grow there eventually, the land can be reclaimed. Both foresters and environmentalists agreed that land subdivision, development, and sprawl consumes the land forever and is the greatest threat to the region.

During my travels many people pointed out that private timberlands in the Northern Forest have long served the local people as de facto parks. The arrangement was in many ways ideal—the timber companies owned the land, the public had access, and both avoided the hassles of dealing with state or federal bureaucracies. This arrangement worked well for generations, and there was little reason for change, for while the companies bought and sold each other's lands from time to time, few people seriously thought the industry would ever let valuable woodlands slip into the hands of a developer. If the timber industry allowed that to happen, people reasoned, they would only be hurting themselves. After all, you can't have a timber industry without healthy forests.

Yet that's exactly what happened to the Diamond International timberlands in the 1980s, when British financier Sir James Goldsmith gobbled up the Diamond International Corporation in a hostile takeover, then proceeded to dismantle the company and sell off parts of its vast timber holdings to developers for enormous profits.

Although most of the Diamond land was eventually purchased by other timber corporations, and the state governments scrambled to acquire what they could, thousands of acres were sold to developers who saw a huge market for prime waterfront lots and vacation home sites.

The Diamond sale was like an alarm going off, and it prompted the federal government to launch the Northern Forest Lands Study that, when completed in 1989, announced what everyone had just learned—that the region and the way of life it supported was threatened by land fragmentation and development. Since the study came out, massive land sales have continued to rock the Northern Forest. Between 1998 and 2001, more than six million acres of forest lands were auctioned off by the paper companies that owned them. Subdivision, home construction, and road building have increased dramatically, jeopardizing irreplaceable lakeshores and other highly scenic areas.

The Northern Forest is being discovered. New technology makes it possible for people to commute electronically to work, and as cities and suburbs become increasingly congested and unlivable, many will relocate to live among these mountains, forests, and lakes. Major infrastructure projects such as the widening of the Maine turnpike and the resumption of rail service between Boston and Portland are facilitating faster and easier access to areas once considered remote. With the nation edging toward a population of 300 million people, many folks I spoke to fear much of the Northern Forest will inevitably be transformed into woodland suburbs, a makeover that will damage the environment, wreck the region's sense of solitude and open space, and destroy any hope for restoring a sustainable forest products industry.

Fortunately, there are signs that all is not yet lost, that there is a growing consensus among all parties that the forest and the unique way of life it supports must be saved for the future. To this end, local communities are using their "Yankee ingenuity" to help protect the landscape and restore its rural and undeveloped character for the benefit of all. Using innovative tools such as conservation easements, large-scale private purchases, and multistate, public-private conservation partnerships, hundreds of thousands of acres across the Northern Forest have been permanently protected by the people who live, work, and recreate here.

As I traveled through the region, I witnessed a growing recognition that if development were allowed to destroy the unique wild character of the forest, the distinctive human spirit of the region would be irretrievably lost as well, for the two are inseparably intertwined. In Howard Frank Mosher's novel

Disappearances, set in the forests of Vermont's Northeast Kingdom, Wild Bill Bonhomme laments:

There are no men like my father in Kingdom County today. They have disappeared as irrevocably as the small family farms and the log drives and the big woods. Such men required room, both physically and spiritually, and even in Kingdom County that room is no longer available. They needed space in which to get away from people and towns and farms and highways, and other people needed space to get away from them since authentic characters are not the easiest persons to live with. To live in a world without them, though, while it is certainly easier, sometimes seems intolerable.

A hiker crosses the rocky summit of Camel's Hump, Green Mountains, Vermont.

OVERLEAF:
Rocky summits of the Presidential Range rise above the clouds on a late-autumn morning in the White Mountains, New Hampshire.

17

NATIVE HIGHWAYS

THE NORTHERN FOREST CANOE TRAIL

The canoe is coming to the front, and canoeing is gaining rapidly in popular favor, in spite of the disparaging remark that "a canoe is a poor man's yacht." But, suppose it is the poor man's yacht? Are we to be debarred from aquatic sports because we are not rich? And are we such weak flunkies as to be ashamed of poverty? Or to attempt shams and subterfuges to hide it? For myself, I freely accept the imputation. In common with nine-tenths of my fellow citizens I am poor—and the canoe is my yacht, as it would were I a millionaire.

—George W. Sears (Nessmuk), *Woodcraft* (1884)

There is no better way to recapture the spirit of an era than to follow the old trails, gathering from the earth itself the feelings and challenges of those who trod them long ago," wrote Sigurd Olson in his essay "Stream of the Past." "The landscape and way of life may be changed, but the same winds blow on waterways, plains, and mountains, the rains, snows, and the sun beat down, the miles are just as long."

Dipping my paddle into a perfect reflection of the autumn sky, watching the clouds swirl around the vortex and spin away, I ponder Olson's words, which I had re-read by the flickering light of last night's campfire. Here on this Native American highway now called the Raquette River, Olson's message seems especially relevant.

Rob Center and Kay Henry canoeing the Clyde River, in Vermont's Northeast Kingdom.

21

The Raquette, which crosses part of New York's Adirondack Park, is an ancient travel route and a small section of a far-flung network of interconnected waterways used by the Iroquois and Algonquian Indians for millennia.

Thousands of years before the Pyramids were built, trade goods, war parties, emissaries, and prophets traveled up and down this wilderness highway. Much later, when the lumbermen cut down the magnificent Adirondack forests, the Raquette was used to drive the logs down to the mills in Tupper Lake. And for the past hundred years or so the river has been a travel corridor for a variety of users, including artists, fishermen, hunters, guides, philosophers, and recreational paddlers.

A few yards off to my right, Rob Center and Kay Henry paddle their tandem eighteen-foot-long tripping canoe. The sleek craft is loaded with camping equipment and supplies for our three-day journey down the Raquette. The former chief executives of the Mad River Canoe Company, Rob and Kay recently made the transition from building canoes to using them as vehicles for enjoying and protecting our natural heritage. When they sold the company a couple of years ago they began to put their energies into their new organization, the Northern Forest Canoe Trail (NFCT).

"The intent behind the trail is to renew the bonds between people and rivers in the Northern Forest," Rob told me when the three of us planned this trip and discussed the goals of the NFCT. "And the way we wanted to do it was by working with a broad coalition of individuals and organizations to reestablish portions of the incredible network of native travel routes as a single long-distance recreational trail, the water version of the Appalachian Trail, a trail which would be a reminder of the history and heritage of this region."

Rob and Kay went on to tell me that in the 1980s Mike Kreppnew, a Maine guide, discovered that the old canoe routes linking the Adirondacks and northern Maine not only still exist, but many are still wild, offering the traveler a real opportunity to, as Olson says, "recapture the spirit of an era."

"The old canoe routes still connect every major river drainage in the northeast," said Kay. "When Kreppner got out the maps and started linking the native trails, he was able to put together a 740-mile-long waterway between Old Forge, New York, and Fort Kent, Maine."

Today the route for the NFCT is a gem, an epic route of natural grandeur and human vitality. It traverses the Northern Forest across four states and links some of the country's most famous waterways, including Lake Champlain, the Connecticut River, the Rangeley Lakes, and the Allagash Wilderness Waterway.

"Paddling the entire trail can take from four to eight weeks and requires all the skills a canoeist can muster," says Rob. "Flat water, white water, portaging, poling, going both upriver and down—the traveler will need to handle it all. For those less experienced or lacking time for a complete passage there are many sections of the trail suitable for shorter, less demanding trips."

The NFCT is not strictly a wilderness journey. By design it flows through villages such as Saranac Lake, New York; Island Pond, Vermont; and Jackman, Maine. It also passes the remnants of communities that no longer exist. Remote Burton Island, in Lake Champlain, was a farm and cow pasture in the nineteenth century. Evidence of the islands' history is scattered throughout the woods and fields where bits of fencing, ancient farming tools, and old stone foundations can still be found. On the portage trail between Chamberlain Lake and Eagle Lake on the Allagash Wilderness Wa-terway, two full-scale steam locomotives stand incongruously in the dark forest, stranded some seventy-five miles from the nearest railroad. Brought here in pieces and assembled on the spot, they hauled logs over the height-of-land starting in 1927, but were used for only a couple of seasons.

Every inch of the NFCT has been used as a travel route for millennia. But that doesn't mean it is tame or easy. The trail incorporates several grueling historic portages over heights-of-land separating watersheds, it traverses wilderness lakes far from the nearest settlements, and it ascends and descends rapid rivers and streams where you are completely dependent upon your wits and skills with a paddle. Indeed, what makes the NFCT such a classic journey is that it cuts a clean cross-section right through the heart of the region's natural and cultural treasures, reconnecting us with the earth and with the past.

"Traversing the NFCT is not just a long-distance lark," says Kay. "It's a journey through the history of the Northern Forest. Everything you see along the way tells a story. History is revealed around each bend in the river."

A canoeist portages around Allagash Falls, Allagash Wilderness Waterway, Maine.

The next morning dawns bright and clear, with a fresh, invigorating breeze flowing down from nearby Canada. As we load the canoes and get under way, I feel the way I often do on a canoe trip: that this is exactly what I should be doing, and exactly where I should be doing it. I feel a tinge of sympathy for those who are office bound on such a beautiful day, but the regretful thought quickly passes as Rob draws my attention to an osprey passing swiftly overhead, riding on the wind. We stop paddling and watch as the big raptor swoops low, and then pulls up and begins to hover high above the river, evidently watching unsuspecting fish in the shallows. Just when the bird seems poised to dive and strike, he flaps and moves on. A moment later we dip our paddles and we too resume our journey, grateful for another one of those magic episodes when the cares of this weary world feel far away and all seems as it should be. Our boat-to-boat banter picks up again, and before long several river miles have slipped silently beneath our hulls.

Central to this NFCT experience is the travel vehicle itself—the canoe. The late Canadian filmmaker Bill Mason has said, "The canoe is the simplest, most functional, yet aesthetically pleasing object ever created," and now as I settle into the rhythm of the day's paddling, I have no quarrel with that assessment. As I reach forward I catch the water with the laminated wood paddle blade, and when I pull on the paddle shaft, the canoe shoots forward. Paddling at the leisurely rate of thirty or forty strokes per minute, I maintain forward momentum as the vessel slices across the water toward our distant goal downstream.

For perhaps the thousandth time I marvel at the elegance and grace of the canoe as a form of transportation, perfectly suited to this region of lakes, rivers, and streams. As my muscles loosen and warm to the day's task, I feel a great deal in common with one who preceded me on this historic waterway: "And I commence with the canoe because that is about the first thing you need on entering the Northern wilderness," wrote George W. Sears, a nineteenth-century Adirondack explorer who under the pen name Nessmuk chronicled his adventures in *Forest and Stream* magazine.

"What the mule or mustang is to the plainsman," he continued, "the boat or canoe is to guide, hunter or tourist who proposes a sojourn in the Adirondacks. And this is why I propose to mention at some length this matter of canoeing and boating. Being . . . a good canoeman, having the summer before me, designing to haunt the nameless lakes and streams not down on the maps, and not caring to hire a guide. . . ." As I paddle I imagine that the river hasn't changed much since Nessmuk's day and that he would probably be a good traveling companion.

As elegant as canoes can be on the water, sooner or later on most NFCT expeditions the time comes when you must carry your vessel and equipment overland. That moment arrives for us when we reach Raquette Falls. Rather than attempt to paddle the mile-long series of waterfalls in fully-loaded boats, we portage.

Voices in the Forest

My father was a guide and the caretaker of a great camp on Saranac Lake until he was ninety-three. At ninety-three he was still walking a mile to the lake and rowing three miles to the camp. And then in the evening he would reverse the trip. He did it every day until he died rowing home in a storm. My brother and I found him floating in the lake. He loved the woods. The money wasn't there, but the satisfaction in doing a good job was there for him. And that mattered most. 🌿

CLARENCE PETTY, *ninety-six-year-old lifelong resident of the Adirondacks and one of the original wilderness planners of the Adirondack Park.*

Years ago, I learned that it's not the *weight* of the packs or the canoe that really makes portaging painful, it's the *length of time* the load is pressing on your shoulders. And so I try to cross each carry as quickly as possible, covering the

Voices in the Forest

The Northern Forest is more than a forest for growing trees. There is a spiritual and a romantic aspect to it, the whole concept of the North Country, from the Allagash to Alaska. And that's where the canoe comes in—it's the best way to get into the country. It's important for people to know the country is still there. It's also important ecologically. The Northern Forest is such a special place for spiritual renewal in an industrial and overpopulated world. It's a place to get a connection back to the planet.

JERRY STELMOK, *builder of hand-made canoes and author of* Building the Maine Guide Canoe *and* The Wood & Canvas Canoe.

distance with a swift-footed shuffle. With canoe on my shoulders and pack on my back, I begin to jog through the woods. Staying loose, keeping my knees slightly bent, I watch out for roots, rocks, and slippery places on the rough trail. I can hear the thunder of the falls off to my left. Suddenly, just when it seems I must stop and rest, I glimpse water glittering through the tree trunks. The sight gives me a shot of energy, and I make it to the end of the carry.

Late at night in camp below the roar of Raquette Falls, I watch the campfire flames flicker and go out. Lying on the bank high above the river, I marvel at my good fortune, for just being here is a priceless gift. The soft forest duff beneath my sleeping bag, the bright stars overhead, the barred owl hooting from the white pine branches across the river, and the cool night air are all extravagant luxuries. The fatigue that now settles over me is pure euphoria, and all told I feel rich beyond belief. And then I realize that thanks to the NFCT, I not only have more of the same to look forward to in the days ahead, but that each day, each bend in the river, will reveal another chapter in the river's story. I roll over and look at my canoe with real affection.

THE GUIDE'S RIVER

I was not prepared for the St. John River. The river I imagined would have been river enough, but the real one, the actual St. John, is awesome and inspiring. How could it, unaltered, be here still in the northeastern United States?

—JOHN MCPHEE, *The Keel of Lake Dickey*

The stream is shallow, the route complex, so I stand up in the stern of the canoe to get a better look ahead. With my polarized sunglasses on, I can see through

the dazzling, dancing light on top of the water to the gravel bottom a few inches beneath the surface. The view is not encouraging.

"Okay, looks like we'll have to get out the lines," I say to my wife and paddling partner, Mary.

She stows her paddle, grabs the bow painter line, and steps out of the canoe. I do the same, grabbing the stern painter. The motions are smooth, well rehearsed. We have been through this procedure at least a dozen times already this afternoon. In the canoe behind ours, John Latterell and Greg Zutz, friends from Minnesota, step out of their canoe and grab their lines as well.

Whitewater kayakers tackle the West Branch of the Penobscot River below Mount Katahdin, Maine.

The water reaches about halfway to the top of our L.L. Bean boots. Grasping the thin lines attached to the deck plates at either end of the seventeen-foot-long tripping canoe, we walk alongside the vessel in the shallows, guiding it through little chutes and around rocks with the ropes. Unencumbered by our weight, the canoe floats freely in four or five inches of water, responding quickly to our commands as we tug on the twenty-foot-long polypropylene lines. This process of forward motion is called lining and, having either used the lines or the ash setting poles for at least half the distance traveled today, we are becoming expert at these shallow-water forms of canoe locomotion.

The stream, which appears to be more rock than water, is one of the major headwaters of the St. John River in far northern Maine. The time of year is late May. The ice went out of the headwater lakes a little over two weeks ago, and we can see places along the banks where the huge ice blocks bulldozed the shore and scraped the bark off the trees. At about the same time as the ice broke up, a late snowstorm dropped several inches of wet snow, adding volume to the spring freshet. And yet, today the water is running out as if someone had pulled the plug. As the water level drops before our eyes, we speculate that there may not be enough water left to make the main river run from Baker Lake to Allagash Village up on the Canadian border.

The St. John is one of the last great free-flowing wild rivers in the country, and the longest river in the Northeast. Beginning northwest of Moosehead Lake, not far from the Quebec border, the St. John flows north, and then east, for more than 200 miles before entering New Brunswick. From there it flows another 200 miles to the Bay of Fundy. The section we are paddling consists of approximately 130 miles of mostly fast water punctuated regularly by challenging rapids. Draining more than 2,700 miles of virtually uninhabited territory, the St. John is by any measure one of the premier canoe-camping river trips in the United States.

On St. John the Baptist's Day in 1604, the French explorer Samuel de Champlain sailed into the mouth of the St. John on the coast of New Brunswick, some 450 miles from our present location, and gave the river its present name. Too bad. The Abenaki had a better name for the river: Wallastook, which means, simply but accurately, "the beautiful river."

American loggers penetrated the St. John watershed in the middle of the nineteenth century, floating tall white pines to mills far downstream. French Canadian settlers followed the loggers into the valley and established farms, providing the logging camps with food for the men and forage for the draft horses. The settlement lasted until the early years of the twentieth century. But when the big trees were exhausted and logging in the St. John watershed ceased to be profitable, the villages disappeared. Today, cleared fields and foundations remain; you can still stumble upon old barrel hoops and rusted wagon wheels in the overgrown meadows, but the buildings are all gone. Logging for spruce and fir has resumed in the watershed, but these days the logs are moved overland by truck.

Although the St. John has never enjoyed the same level of protection afforded its more famous neighbor, the Allagash, in the past few years several groundbreaking conservation initiatives have been put in place to protect some 530,000 acres of forestland in the upper St. John region, as well as another 656,000 acres in the West Branch of the Penobscot region—including Baker Lake and the St. John Ponds. These public-private partnerships will preserve the region from development; ensure that sustainable forest management continues in the watershed; and safeguards public access for fishing, paddling, hunting, and hiking for generations to come.

To our relief, the river is deeper ahead. Soon the water is knee-high. "Looks good from here," says Mary. "Let's paddle or pole." With the same smooth motions we used getting out of the canoe we reverse the process and get back in. We are getting used to the drill. I get out the setting pole and push the canoe ahead until the water is deep enough to paddle.

A mile later the river is the color of dark tea—and deep. Narrow, only a canoe's length wide, the flow twists and turns through a thick tangle of spruce and fir. Snarls of alder crowd the banks, reducing our view and weaving a lattice of vegetation. Old beaver dams flood back channels, braiding the river into a knot. Which way do we go? We start down one channel until it ends, abruptly, in a jumbled barricade of blown-down spruce trees. We can hear the river pouring through the entwined branches and crisscrossed trunks, but there is no path for us in here.

And so we back out. John and Greg, seeing us retreat, choose another channel. A few serpentine turns and they too are halted by blowdowns. This time, though, it is only a couple of large trees blocking our path. "No problem," says John, "We can just lift everything over and keep on going." He's right. With four people, lifting the two canoes over the log jam is easy. Soon we are across and back on our way.

As the river widens again to a canoe length or so, we hear the sound of a large animal crashing through the woods just downstream. When we round the

A canoe at sunset on Long Lake, Adirondack Park, New York.

next bend we pull abreast of a sandbar covered with fresh moose tracks. The big, wet, cloven prints lead up to the alder thicket and vanish. Ahead, the river has also vanished. Puzzled, we stop and drift on the flat water of a deep dark pond, our paddles resting on the gunwales.

At one end of the pond we can see a flat, horizontal line—but nothing beyond. As we drift in silence, we hear a rhythmic gulping sound coming from somewhere beyond the line. We drift a few yards more, and then we see a wide, flat opening where the huge beaver dam holding back the main river channel has been breached.

The river pours over this break, sliding down the face of the dam in a perfectly smooth, undulating glassy chute, dropping four or five feet to the deep pool below. Anticipating a good ride, we head straight for the opening, slide through the gap, and drop down the face of the dam just like flume logs at an amusement park, each canoe landing with a bright splash below.

Below the dam the river becomes shallow again, and once more we must get out and line the boats, this time for more than an hour. By midafternoon we have only covered half the distance to Baker Lake. We have had enough lining practice. If there were a world championship, I would enter with confidence. I am more than ready to start paddling and can feel my patience wearing thin as I splash through the shallows.

From time to time we stop for a handful of peanuts or a drink of water, and then keep going. Lining is slow, technical work, and we aren't moving fast enough to cover as much ground as we need to. With evening approaching, I keep an eye out for possible campsites, but the thick brush and swampy ground aren't appealing and offer only the promise of a wet, buggy spot for the night. Although none of us has openly mentioned the possibility of not reaching our goal for the day, the possibility of having to bivouac back here looms larger as the sun makes its slow transit across the sky.

Scanning the brilliant sunlit surface of the river, letting out more line and tugging to guide the canoe to deeper water, I remind myself that we are here because we choose to be. All four of us are or have been professional wilderness guides and trip leaders. John and Greg, Boundary Waters veterans, have come all the way from Minnesota to experience this legendary waterway. With no students or clients to watch out for, we can learn from the river and from each other, and the St. John is the perfect classroom. This is a guide's river, a place to hone all of our wilderness canoe-tripping skills, and that includes route finding, poling, and lining.

We are a little surprised by the continuous blowdowns, beaver dams, back channels, and shallows. But we expected some, and in a perverse way have even come searching for them. The St. John is still a wild, spirited river, and hazards and obstructions come with the territory. Anything less and we would be disappointed. There are plenty of tame, uninspiring waterways in the world to paddle, but there is only one St. John.

Sometime later a small stream enters the river from the right bank. Greg stops and gets out the map. He studies it for a while, checks his compass, and then looks around to match the nondescript features of the landscape to what he sees on the map. "Must be Campbell Brook," he says after a while, confirming what we all hope to hear. "Maybe a mile more of this, and then we hit the swamp and deeper water."

With renewed hope comes renewed energy, and we pick up the pace, sloshing through the shallows and brushing aside the overhanging branches that rip at our shirts and hats. The swamp will mean deep, meandering loops and oxbows, progress will probably be maddeningly slow—most likely we will have to paddle three miles of looping river to make just one mile of forward progress—but at least we will be able to get in a rhythm and will feel as though we are making progress. And we just may arrive at Baker Lake tonight.

OVERLEAF: *A whitewater kayaker immersed in the "Cribworks," a challenging rapid on the West Branch of the Penobscot River, Maine.*

The sun continues to slant toward the horizon and the western sky takes on a rich amber glow as we get back in the canoes and paddle in earnest. Soon a golden path stretches across the depthless water from us to the setting sun. As colors and details fade, shapes and sounds take on added significance, and I watch the ragged black line of spruce etched against the sky or the silhouette of the other canoe defined by the backdrop of molten water. From back in the slough we can hear waves splash against an unseen shore. A loon calls with a haunting cry, and then another answers from somewhere in the far distance. A gust of wind bends the treetops. The waves are louder now; they must be just around the bend. As the horizon and the sun collide, we emerge onto Baker Lake.

Relieved, we drift gunwale to gunwale in the low rolling swells, looking down the long wilderness lake. Scanning the eastern shore with my binoculars, peering into the falling dark, I locate the campsite a mile or so in the distance. End in sight, we paddle hard until we get there, and in half-an-hour the tents and the tarp are up, there is a cheerful fire of dry split spruce crackling, and the dinner pots are heating on the grill. After a long hard day of river bushwhacking, we have made it to open water—from here on down to the junction with the Allagash it looks like we'll be able to ride the river's current. As I look over

An expedition canoeist relaxes by the campfire, Maine Woods.

the snug camp, at the canoes overturned above the bank, at the fire snapping, at my companions, I have a solid familiar feeling of accomplishment and self-sufficiency, and despite the sweat and toil it took to get here, I'm exactly where I want to be.

As the light leaves the sky and the sparkling stars of the Milky Way emerge from the black dome overhead, I wander down to the water's edge and look out over miles of dark, empty shoreline. I can smell the wood smoke and hear the others around the fire, chatting excitedly about the day and about the river days to come. After a while John comes over with a couple of steaming mugs of hot chocolate laced with something bracing from our "snake-bite kit."

"So, was it worth it?" he asks, grinning.

THE BIG DROP

Many people who saw the riverman only in his worst moments—that is, in town after the drive was in, unkempt, drunk, roaring, and fighting—forgot or never knew that those moments of violent relaxation formed only three weeks out of fifty-two in the man's hard life. It was pretty apparent that a riverman was strong in the back, but most people thought he must be weak in the head.

—ROBERT E. PIKE, *Tall Trees, Tough Men*

OVERLEAF: *A rushing stream pours over a rocky ledge in the Adirondack Park, New York.*

My stern partner Ed Green ties the canoe to a large rock on shore with the bow painter. It is late afternoon on a chilly, slate-colored day in May. Now and then the skies let loose with a cold lashing rain, and the big black river is still frigid with the ice and snowmelt of winter. We are both damp and tired from a long day of scouting and running tough rapids, but we still have a few miles to paddle to our take-out.

There is a persistent rumbling sound, like a convoy of heavily loaded semi-trucks crossing a plank bridge coming from around the bend down-stream. The wind shifts and a fine damp mist, like wave spume on a windy day at the beach, drifts upstream and over us, adding to the penetrating chill we already feel.

Though we can't see around the bend, we know where we are. The blind corner, the thunder, the heavy pounding vibration tells us we are at

Nesowadnehunk Falls, or "Soudyhunk," as the locals call it, on the West Branch of the Penobscot River in northern Maine.

The ancient portage trail around the horseshoe-shaped falls leads up and over a high rocky ledge on river left. Leaving the canoe, we stretch our cold, cramped muscles and scramble up for a better look. As we top the rise, the falls come in to view below us, and the rumbling grows louder until we must shout to communicate.

"No way," I lean over and holler near Ed's ear while looking at the falls below. "Not this one." The entire brawling river is leaping and churning through a set of roiling rapids before plunging over an eight-foot drop. Not only that, but there is a haystack-sized standing wave leaping skyward at the bottom of the pitch. "Even if we make it through the rapids and over the big drop," I shout and point, "that standing wave will eat us alive. There's no way we can get through that in an open canoe!"

Ed doesn't hear me. He's concentrating, and his eyes are narrow slits glinting with excitement.

I look back at the falls, trying to see what Ed is looking at, hoping he's not contemplating running this pitch. Already today we have run Big Ambejackmockamus, and the Horse Race, and several other legendary West Branch rapids. And now, as we watch this scale-model Niagara, which my paddler's guidebook says is "unrunnable," I suddenly realize that I know a story about this very spot. Even though I have never been here before, I'm certain this is the place. It all fits, and the sense of recognition jolts me like a mild electric shock.

In college I had taken a course in American folklore, and some of the tales that most captured my imagination were about loggers in the Great North Woods. One of the stories was about a big, tough 260-pound Native American woodsman named Big Sebattis Mitchell, a real-life folk hero who worked on the West Branch drive back in the 1870s during the long-log days when the big white pines were floated down to the mills in Bangor.

The Penobscot River men called themselves the Bangor Tigers, and they were the best river drivers the world has ever seen. Logging companies all across the country sought their services. According to one story, a logging executive in Minnesota was watching his crews on a river drive one day when he noticed a particularly able young man dancing nimbly from log to log in the white water, picking jams and generally doing the work of several men. When the boss called the young man over and asked him where he was from, the river driver took a bite from his plug of chewing tobacco, spat, and said, "From the Penobscot, b'God!"

One reason the Penobscot men were so successful at running the logs down turbulent waterways was their quick, responsive watercraft. Designed and built in Old Town and Bangor, the Maynard Bateaux, called "the Great Maynards" by the rivermen, were built for extremely dangerous work picking log jams in the middle of violent rapid rivers. To free a log jam required experience, nerve, and athleticism. It also required a fast, stable boat to paddle up below the jam, pick the key stick holding back hundreds of tons of wood, and paddle away before being crushed to death when the logs came plunging downstream driven by the pent-up force of the river.

The Great Maynards were that kind of nimble boat, and the rivermen called them "catty." But out of the water, the Maynards were anything but lithe dancers. At thirty-two feet long, seven feet wide, and weighing between eight and nine hundred pounds, they were miserable to carry around the many long rapids on the West Branch between Ripogenus Gorge and the junction with the East Branch.

According to Fannie Hardy Eckstorm, who heard the story of Big Sebattis and Soudyhunk Falls from the loggers and later collected it in her classic book *The Penobscot Man,* Big Sebattis decided he was tired of carrying the big, heavy wooden bateau around these rapids. So, Big Sebat, as the other drivers called him, turned to his partner, another Native American handy with a paddle, and suggested trying to run the drop instead of making the brutal portage. His partner agreed, and the two of them decided to go for it. If they made it, they would be famous, legends of the Penobscot drive. If they didn't make it—well, they would give it their best shot.

Whitewater rafters at the point of no-return on a wild river in northern Maine.

The other drivers had already carried their two bateaux around the falls when they suddenly saw Big Sebattis and his partner crashing over the falls. Miraculously still upright, they disappeared down the river and around the bend. The others raced after them and found them calmly taking their ease, smoking their pipes, as if they did this every day.

The other men, twelve in all, were not to be outdone. Pride was at stake, and they promptly marched back to their bateaux, carried them back around the falls to the top, and attempted to run the drop. Both boats were smashed to toothpicks. Eleven of the men managed to swim to shore. The twelfth man drowned.

I turn to Ed. "Have you heard the story about . . ." I start, but he cuts me off. "We can do it," he says. "Look, you see that rooster tail—that tall curling wave right at the top of the falls? As long as we stay right on top of that, we'll be okay. That will be your job. You've got to steer us right over the crest. Otherwise the curl of the wave will flip us over before we even get to the falls!"

If I am supposed to be reassured by this, I am not. But, like a river driver, I am not to be outdone. Besides, I see he has a point. If we line up perfectly, if we hit the crest, we can shoot the rapids and the falls. And if we do it carrying enough speed to crash through the monster standing wave at the bottom of the falls, we'll be all right. It's just that there's no room for error.

The other canoes in our party opt to carry around. They tell us we are

Maneuvering through whitewater on the upper Androscoggin River, New Hampshire.

40

fools but assure us they will pick up the pieces that come floating downstream.

Back in our boat above the rapids, I feel a rush of adrenaline mixed with a hefty dollop of fear. We untie from the rock and paddle hard, angling upstream against the flood to get out into the main current where we can position ourselves to get safely around the blind corner.

"You ready?' yells Ed.

"Let's do it!" I shout back.

And then we turn the canoe and face downstream. The current is violent. It catches the hull and sweeps the boat swiftly toward the chaos ahead. Racing forward, we clear the corner and now I can see the spray hanging in the air above the waterfall. The roar of the falls and the strength of the current intensify as we hurtle toward the edge. My senses are bombarded. I remember to take a deep breath and use my paddle. "This is insane," I think.

In the bedlam I remember to look for the curling rooster tail wave, knowing that if we don't line up properly, we won't have a chance. Scanning ahead, I try to pick it out but I can't see it! The river looks completely different from down here at water level than it did from high above. "Focus," I tell myself, then, "Breathe."

At the last possible moment I see the rooster-tail. It's just ahead and to the right. I react with a quick, powerful crossbow draw and the boat pulls over sharply, aiming right for the top of the curling wave. "Way to go!" shouts Ed, and then we shoot right over the lip.

Time and canoe hang suspended as we free-fall for at least a full second, but it seems much longer. We slide downward violently on the rushing water, then crash right into the trough beneath the towering wave. The canoe seems to shudder, almost stops, but then punches on through. The wave has gone completely over my head. We are soaked; the canoe is filled and is pitching from side to side and threatening to capsize. But we are upright. We made it!

From the bank a loud cheer goes up where the vultures were watching. Ed and I gingerly paddle the wallowing boat to shore, and when we get there our erstwhile companions slap our backs, give us high-fives, and congratulate us on our daring and on our paddling skills. Ed and I feel like modern folk heroes of the Penobscot.

As we empty out the boat, I turn to the others and say, "Hey, have you guys heard the story of Big Seb . . ." But they aren't there. Not to be outdone, they are carrying their canoes back to the top of the falls.

A RUMOR OF WOLVES

Snow falls thickly from an ashen sky. It's been snowing for three days now, and with no wind, the dime-size flakes drift softly earthward with a mesmerizing effect. They pile one atop the other, adding their feathery shapes to the geology of the snowpack.

Four or five feet of the white stuff cloak the rocks, stumps, and downed trees of the forest floor. I am sitting on a snowy log, eating a quick lunch of crackers and cheese. A ribbon of smoke rises from the cup of hot chocolate in my gloved hand.

Looking around, I notice that off to my left a section of woods has been removed by loggers, and a skidder trail twitches through the stumps to where it rejoins the main logging road about a quarter-mile away. This place is the Perry Stream valley in far northern New Hampshire, very close to the border with Quebec.

I get up, toss on my pack, and turn away from the cutting site. Ahead, a blur of muted color breaks from the trees. It's Jeff Fair, wildlife biologist. He's on snowshoes, following the track of some animal. Fair stops, peers keenly for a moment at the snow, scribbles a note, then moves on. I catch up and fall in behind him, partly because he is more expert in the art of tracking than I am, but mostly to let him break trail through the heavy drift.

There are many tracks in this section of forest. We cross the delicate signatures of fox, fisher, and red squirrel. A little while later we intersect a set of erratic, lunging craters in the snow left by a moose. Our own snowshoes—traditional wooden modified bearpaws—leave a very pleasing trail. We follow

Wolves were once plentiful in the Northern Forest, but by the early 1900s they had been eliminated from the region.

43

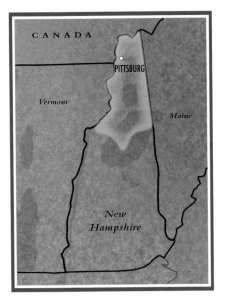

the distinctive offset track of a pine marten for a while, and then enter another cutting site where, Jeff tells me, a pile of drifted-over slash might shelter a hibernating black bear. Quietly, we poke around a bit, trying to determine if anyone is at home down there under the snow.

As the pale afternoon light fades, Jeff and I recall that we have business here. We are not in Perry Stream to check up on the coyotes, deer, bear, moose, grouse, and other creatures great and small struggling to make their living here in these cold, snowy woods. We are actually in this overlooked corner of New England chasing a phantom. We are here investigating a rumor of wolves.

We enter an area of intense deer activity, a yard where the snow has been beaten down to pavement by their sharp hooves. This is where the gaunt animals wait out the long, difficult winter beneath the sheltering canopy of a thick stand of conifers. In short order Jeff and I jump half a dozen scrawny deer. The animals are desperately hungry, and we find pine saplings chewed to nubbins. Some young trees, slightly taller and tufted with needles at their tops, are so gnawed they look like spindly bottle washers.

Jeff picks up a coyote track. These animals, once native only to the Southwest, are now firmly established in the Northern Forest. Here, they fill the role of top predator, a position once occupied in these woods by the timber wolf.

The coyote track brings back the memory of a bitter-cold January day on the frozen West Branch of the Penobscot River in northern Maine. Friends and I were in the middle of a week-long snowshoe expedition from Northeast Carry to Caucomgomoc Lake. On that day I was out in front of the group breaking trail through heavy snow when I heard ravens croak, then saw the big black birds flap away from me, heading downriver and out of sight.

When I rounded a bend I saw two large eastern coyotes staring at me. They were about fifty yards away, and they were huge—the size of German shepherds, perhaps seventy pounds. I was startled at their appearance because they were so much bigger than the many western coyotes I had seen on trips through sagebrush country. I stopped in my tracks and stared back at them. The animals looked almost as much like wolves as coyotes, which was not surprising because northern New England's coyotes are predominantly wolf-coyote hybrids.

The animals bounded across the ice to the thick cover of the spruce trees, leaving behind the full-grown deer they had killed. Partially eaten, the deer was still warm when I reached it. The tracks in the snow told the timeless story of how the coyotes had chased the deer out of the forest and onto the ice where they had used their agility, skill, and teamwork to bring the deer down.

Though they are merely filling the role nature designed for them, the rank of top predator is a heavy burden for coyotes. On trips through the North Country I have listened to otherwise perfectly reasonable men and women accuse the animals of premeditated wickedness, of moral depravity, as if coyotes were the Charles Mansons of the animal kingdom. One man in northern Maine showed me a grisly collection of fourteen dead coyotes, his body count through midwinter. He had trapped and strangled the animals with piano wire snares. The stiff, furry forms were stacked like logs on a blue tarpaulin in his basement.

One man in northern Maine showed me a grisly collection of dead coyotes. He had trapped and strangled the animals with piano wire snares.

Fair and I break out of the forest and enter a beaver meadow, where we rendezvous with John Harrigan, the third member of our small party. Opinionated, yet personable and outgoing, Harrigan is a North Country newspaper publisher, and he keeps his ear to the ground. One thing he has been hearing lately is this: a strange creature, a large, black canine, has been seen haunting the woods in the vicinities of Indian Stream and Perry Stream.

Harrigan didn't dismiss these stories out of hand, even though the last known wolf in New Hampshire was shot in 1887. Instead, he explored Indian Stream on foot, and he found a den. He took notes and measurements and later described what he had found to a friend, a biologist for the United States Fish and Wildlife Service. When Harrigan finished, the biologist told him he had just described the den of a wolf.

Wolves are essentially large wild dogs—in fact, they are the original dog. Some 12,000 years ago, humans began domesticating wild wolves and putting them to work. Today all dogs, from Great Danes to dachshunds, are closely related to, and direct descendents of, the wild wolf.

One difference between wolves and dogs is that there is no record of anyone ever being killed by a wild wolf in the wilderness of North America. Domestic dogs, on the other hand, do sometimes turn on their owners and others. Although the incidents are relatively rare, domestic dogs are involved in hundreds of attacks on people each year in the United States. Some twenty people are killed annually in this country by domestic dogs. But whereas dogs rightfully enjoy their status as "man's best friend," wolves continue to suffer from our misplaced fears and suspicions.

Jeff Fair and John Harrigan talking to a logger about a potential wolf sighting in northern New Hampshire.

Wolves were once plentiful here in the Northern Forest. Indeed, wolves were once the most widely distributed mammal in the Northern Hemisphere. For millennia they co-existed with the moose, deer, caribou, beaver, and other animals that formed their prey base in this region. But from the time of the arrival of Europeans to these shores, wolves were profoundly affected by human activities. Bounty hunting, habitat destruction, and depletion of prey populations took a serious toll on their numbers. By the early 1900s wolves were completely gone from the Northern Forest.

The disappearance of the timber wolf is symptomatic of the loss of wilderness in the Northern Forest region. The top carnivore, and a species whose presence is a good indication of ecological well-being, the timber wolf requires healthy forest ecosystems to survive. That the wolf is not currently present in the Northern Forest suggests the forest ecosystem is incomplete and out of equilibrium. The explosive growth of prey species, including moose and deer, is evidence of this imbalance.

Prior to European settlement, moose were more common than deer in the Northern Forest. And though wolves were also plentiful in precolonial times, for millennia the moose and the wolf maintained a balance. But by 1900, the wolf was a memory and the moose too faced extirpation from overhunting. At the turn of the twentieth century fewer than two thousand moose wandered the forests of Maine, and there were fewer than fifteen moose left in all of New Hampshire.

When strict hunting regulations were put in place in the early decades of the twentieth century, the moose population began a very slow rebound. Moose numbers remained small all across the Northern Forest until the 1970s, when large-scale mechanized clear-cutting began in earnest. Then, the new harvesting practices began creating huge swaths of succulent young browse where mature forests had once stood. The animals took advantage of this nutritional windfall, and during the next two decades the moose population grew exponentially.

With the wolf gone and no other large predators to help keep their numbers in check, the moose herd in northern New England is currently estimated at more than 40,000 animals and still growing rapidly. And though the large gawky animals are popular with tourists, the high moose numbers are also a burden.

In the three states—Maine, New Hampshire, and Vermont—where moose are common, the animals are involved in hundreds of motor-vehicle collisions yearly. Some of these crashes result in human fatalities, and they exact a huge economic toll. For example, according to the Maine Department of Inland Fisheries and Wildlife, there were 2,126 moose-vehicle collisions in the state between 1996 and 1998. In those crashes 637 people were injured, including 8 people killed. The estimated economic impact of those collisions was a whopping fifty million dollars.

Moose also give farmers fits. The huge creatures break down fences and free livestock. They run through maple sugar tubing and spill valuable sap—an important source of seasonal income in the north. They also trample the gardens of Boston suburbanites, and they wander down into Connecticut, where moose are establishing a resident population for the first time since the colonial era. State wildlife management agencies have responded by opening limited hunting seasons in an effort to stabilize their numbers. The moose hunts are popular, and they meet a number of social as well as wildlife management goals, but it's not clear that they have an impact on the actual size of the herd.

Hunter success rates in Maine have been extremely high. For example, in 1991 the state issued 1,000 permits, and hunters bagged 959 animals. Nine

OVERLEAF: *I fall in behind Jeff Fair, partly because he is more expert in the art of tracking than I am, but mostly to let him break trail through the heavy drift.*

years later Maine increased the number of permits to 3,000, and 2,552 hunters were successful. In the meantime, moose watching has blossomed into an important tourist industry, and few who travel the region hoping to see a moose are disappointed.

The flourishing white-tailed deer herd in the Northern Forest is also much larger today than prior to the colonial era. When Europeans first settled in northern New England, the deer herd was largely restricted to coastal regions—moose and woodland caribou occupied the interior. As wolves and caribou were hunted into extinction and the moose were nearly eliminated, the deer herd expanded spectacularly.

Today deer are found throughout the Northern Forest. Like the moose they are popular with both hunters and tourists. But white-tails are also widely considered something of a nuisance. The deer cause devastating agricultural losses totaling millions of dollars each year, they are a critical vector in the spread of Lyme disease, and they are involved in some 3,500 automobile collisions annually in Maine alone. Because wolves prey upon moose and

Captive wolves look out at the world from behind a chainlink fence. Will the cry of the wolf be heard again in the Northern Forest?

deer, perhaps it's no surprise that some conservationists have recently been calling for returning the wolf to the Northern Forest to try and help reinstate a balance. But given the enormous impact of human activities such as logging and land development, it's not clear what, if any, effect wolves would have on the overall size of the moose and deer herds.

Still, for many the notion that the howl of the wolf may someday be heard again in the Northern Forest is exciting. And it's not out of the question. After centuries of trying to eradicate the animal, wolf restoration programs are under way all across the United States. In North Carolina, Wyoming, Idaho, and Arizona, wolves have been reintroduced into the wild. In northern New York and New England there are many people from across the social spectrum who believe that the wolf should be restored here too.

We kick the snow from our boots, climb into the cab of Harrigan's large black four-wheel-drive Ford pick-up truck, then head north on Route 3 through the Connecticut Lakes region as the snow continues to fall. As we drive, Harrigan and Fair, both avid hunters, express their disappointment with the region's state game agencies because they feel the agencies stymie predator reintroduction programs. When I ask why the fish and game departments would interfere, Harrigan and Fair explain that it's because the agencies fear that their constituents—the license-fee-paying hunters—are opposed. Harrigan, who shot a moose the first year New Hampshire re-opened its moose season, will have none of it.

"The agencies assume hunters are against wolves and cougars—not to mention coyotes, fishers, and foxes—because they prey upon animals hunters regard as 'theirs,'" he says. "According to Fish and Game, wolf recovery is 'unfeasible' and 'unjustifiable' politically and economically. That assumption is totally out of step with reality, but it's still presented as 'official policy.' The truth is," Harrigan goes on, "a lot of hunters would really like to see the wolf back here, where it belongs." Fair nods his assent.

"Besides," says Harrigan, getting his dander up just a bit, "are we humans so mercenary that the life or death of a species depends solely on its supposed worth to us? That unless they hold the cure for cancer or Alzheimer's they aren't worth protecting? It seems so. But I believe these animals have a basic right to exist."

Harrigan says he hopes to see the wolf pull an end-run on the system and reestablish itself here in the North Country on its own, without any help from humans, thereby avoiding the political wrangling and divisiveness that accompanies official restoration programs. The chances of that happening may be slim, but it's not impossible. Canadian wolves migrating south into Glacier National Park reestablished themselves as a viable population in the northern Rockies in the 1980s. Minnesota wolves spread into Wisconsin and Michigan and reestablished populations in those states on their own. It could happen here, too, as the events of August 31, 1993, suggest.

On that day a mature black female timber wolf was shot by a bear hunter in the Maine woods west of Baxter State Park. The shooting came as something of a surprise to wildlife managers because the wolf had been officially extinct in Maine for more than a century.

But that dead wolf, and another trapped in eastern Maine in 1996, merely confirmed what many local hunters, guides, and outdoorsmen and women had known for quite a while: that wolves have been turning up in the Northern Forest in recent years. A game warden in northern Maine told me about the wolf that dashed across a logging road right in front of his truck. A wildlife professional, he has no doubt about what he saw. The elusive Perry Stream wolf, and another wolf whose tracks wildlife researchers kept encountering one recent winter in the woods north of Baxter State Park, were other individuals who had probably negotiated the difficult journey down from Quebec.

Paul Matula, Head of Research for the Maine Department of Inland Fisheries and Wildlife, speculated that the wolf shot west of Baxter State Park was a migrant from Quebec. "The Maine woods are within 75 miles of wolf territory in the Quebec Laurentians," he told me when I spoke with him on the telephone. "That's not very far for a young wolf to travel while exploring new territory." Indeed, wolves have been known to use huge areas—1,000 square miles and more. The animals may travel up to 500 miles in search of new range.

Matula mentioned that the animal may have crossed the Saint Lawrence River during the winter. The wolf might then have traveled through the settled agricultural region along the river's south shore to the Maine woods.

"If Canadian wolves knew how much food was available down here, more of them might make the trip," Matula said, citing Maine's deer, moose, and beaver populations that have surged due to lack of predators. He said these animals would provide the wolves with a healthy prey base.

For some reason, perhaps merely the longing to see new country, individual wolves have made the difficult journey across the Saint Lawrence lowlands.

They ran a dangerous gauntlet of settled farms and small villages. But for them the crossing was worth the risk, and others will surely follow. Perhaps Harrigan is right. Perhaps the wolf will establish itself again here, without any help from us.

But if they make the trip, what will they find?

Most importantly, they will find vast areas of unsettled open space. In the Northern Forest there are millions of acres without paved roads, without villages, without dwellings of any kind. There is room here for wolves, cougars, caribou, wolverines, and lynx—animals that once roamed these forests. This is a large unfragmented wildland, perhaps the last best place in the country to attempt ecological restoration on a significant scale. This restoration need not have an adverse impact on humans, for even though logging (along with tourism) has long been the region's economic mainstay, if given the chance wolves would still thrive here in these immense unpopulated reaches. Wolves and people are both prospering in Minnesota's Superior and Chippewa National Forests, where timber harvesting continues at relatively high levels.

Deer capes hang outside a home in Vermont's Northeast Kingdom. According to John Harrigan, many hunters would like to see the wolf back in the Northern Forest where it belongs.

In the meantime, while we humans debate the relative merits and drawbacks of restoration, the wolves keep showing up—here, there, one by one.

Harrigan pulls the truck to a stop next to the snow-swept surface of a frozen lake. We can barely see the dark spruce on the opposite shore through fleeting rifts in the snow.

"This is where the last caribou in New Hampshire were seen in 1905," he says, nodding to the frozen expanse he identifies as Second Connecticut Lake. I look out over the lake through curtains of snow and imagine a pack of wolves shadowing caribou over the soft white surface.

"An old man named Atchison told me about it when I was young," says Harrigan. "He said he saw eleven caribou crossing Second Lake in a snowstorm, on a day just like this. He watched until they vanished in the falling snow. They were the last ones, and they were never seen again."

ISLANDS IN THE MIST

From the Blackwoods campground on Mount Desert Island, the South Ridge Trail climbs the long pink granite slopes of Cadillac Mountain in Acadia National Park, Maine. Breaking free of the cool mixed hardwood forest, I emerge into bright sunshine and blue skies, and I lope along the bare rock shelves and ledges, quickly dissolving the distance between myself and the summit.

After a couple of miles of easy hiking, I take a short side trail out to an overlook, toss off my daypack, and perch on the warm glacier-scoured rock. From on high the view over the ocean is exceptional, and the air is so clear and dry it's like looking through polished glass. An offshore breeze spilling down from the summit caresses my face, picks up speed as it flows downslope, and fills the expansive cream-colored sails of a three-masted schooner a half-mile or so offshore.

An island emerges from the mist in the Deer Isle Thoroughfare, Maine coast.

The vessel comes to life like a giant sea creature stirring from her slumbers. Through my binoculars I can see her canvas billow, her rigging stretch taut, her pennants snap. I imagine I can hear the creaking of wooden blocks and tackle as the ship starts to heel. Minutes later the vessel is sending up sheets of salty spray from her bow as she pitches forward through the swells.

And then several other tall ships glide into view. It's a scene from another century. I watch, transfixed, as the bright sails move among the green islands and against the indigo backdrop of the open Atlantic Ocean.

Moving again, following the cairns of broken stones marking the trail, I recall my own ocean voyages by sea kayak along this coast. There were many days of bright sunshine, favorable winds, and friendly tides. But there were also plenty of fog-bound days of navigating by compass and dead reckoning, and also unforgettable moments when I could hear boat-smashing breakers crashing on islands just yards away. The din swelled and the sea rolled under the hull, but the islands and the rocks remained hidden from view behind thick veils of mist.

✤

THE FIRST EXPLORERS

The vessel comes to life like a giant sea creature stirring from her slumbers. I can see her canvas billow, her rigging stretched taut, her pennants snap.

Giovanni Verrazano made the first recorded sea voyage here when he sailed these waters in 1524. He is also credited with giving the region its name, which came to him from one of two sources. The first possibility is that a native may have used the word "Quoddy," which Verrazano transcribed as "Acadie" to describe the region in a meeting with the explorer. The second possibility is that Verrazano borrowed the word "Arcadia," which describes a pastoral paradise, from classic Greek or Roman works.

The Italian explorer described the coast as scattered with islands "all near the continent; small and pleasant in appearance, but high; following the curve of the land; some beautiful ports and channels formed between them." Reaching for a parallel, he likened the Maine archipelago to the islands of the Adriatic Sea.

Long before Verrazano, the first seafarers to venture out over Maine coastal waters were the Abenaki Indians, who hunted, fished, and foraged here

for at least six thousand years prior to European settlement. Employing birch bark canoes ranging in size from small single-man models to huge vessels capable of carrying a ton or more, the Indians were familiar with all of Maine's islands, even those twenty miles out to sea.

Using the islands as summer encampments, the Abenaki made hunting and fishing excursions into the incredibly rich coastal environment. They gathered molting waterfowl in the marshes; hunted seals, porpoises, and blue-fin tuna offshore; harpooned whales in the deeper bays; plucked lobsters from the spiny reefs; and gathered clams, berries, and roots on the islands themselves.

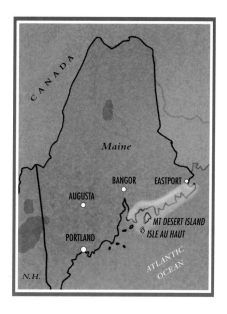

The Abenaki were likely visited by mysterious strangers a thousand years ago, when serpentine long ships bearing bearded, pale-skinned men parted the mists. It appears the Viking explorers merely passed through the islands, stopping neither for trade nor settlement. Perhaps their restless souls searched for a land of riches, for something to plunder. Whatever they found here, it wasn't worth taking, and they quickly disappeared into the gloom, never to be seen again, leaving only riddles in their wake.

Six centuries later, in September of 1604, a little ship flying the fleur-de-lis of France sailed the Gulf of Maine, coasting the shores of a land shrouded in fog and mystery. Under the command of Samuel de Champlain, the little ship sailed along the wild, solitary shore. From the pitching ship's deck the explorers saw bold rocky headlands crowned by thick forests of spruce and fir. Offshore, gleaming granite islands jutted from the cold depths, some rising a thousand feet above the sea, while others merely breached the surface like the backs of whales asleep in the swells.

OVERLEAF: A sea kayaker in camp on a deserted island near Acadia National Park, Maine.

Landing on one of the larger islands, Champlain remarked upon the smooth, sloping mountaintops, and he called it "L'isle des Monts Deserts," "the Island of the bare mountains." (The Abenaki already had a name for the island, calling it "Pemetic," "the sloping land.") Then Champlain named another island off to the west "L'isle au Haut," "the High Island," for the dramatic way it thrust high above the sea. Centuries later, along with the Schoodic Peninsula, Mount Desert Island and Isle au Haut became what is now Acadia National Park.

A DYNAMIC LANDSCAPE

Acadia is a small park. Consisting of only 108 square miles and defined by a roaming boundary weaving in and out of private holdings and incorporating portions of offshore islands and a distant peninsula, Acadia is nevertheless one of the crown jewels of the National Park System. It is a natural province of unsurpassed beauty, a land of astonishing contrasts, a place where rugged mountains and cold northern forests march down to the sea.

Diversity is the theme, and the charm, of Acadia, for the park is an unusual crossroads of mountain and ocean, of northern and temperate climates, of civilization and wilderness. Here, a short hike will take you from the tidal zone to the alpine zone, from the shops of bustling Bar Harbor village to the silent boreal forest. In Acadia, the pungent fragrance of balsam fir blends with the salty tang of the sea. In a single day you may see deer, beaver, sea urchins, porpoises, bald eagles, and whales. Surely no other national park offers a greater diversity of environments and experiences than Acadia.

Mount Desert Island, constituting the bulk of Acadia, lies just off the northern coast of Maine, the portion of the state called "Down East." The term naturally confuses people from "Away" until they learn that in the age of sail, ships heading east from Boston and Portsmouth had the advantage of sailing

Maine lobstermen take a break after a long day on the water hauling traps.

downwind on the prevailing westerly breeze. But perhaps even more remarkable than its name is the actual length of this coastline: Maine possesses fully half the nation's Atlantic shore. Though it measures only 228 miles from east to west, the vagrant Maine Coast winds in and out of a bewildering maze of peninsulas, necks, and islands for some 3,500 miles—a distance far greater than the span between Maine and California.

With its deep bays, inlets, and the only fjord on the U.S. Atlantic coast—Somes Sound—Acadia is typical of this meandering strand and of the sublime beauty of rock and sea. Many visitors are initially entranced by the rugged magnificence of the cliffs fronting the sea, by the arms and fingers of the ocean reaching far inland. Eventually, as they hike the bare summits or clamber over the cobble beaches, some wonder how this unique blend of water and stone came to be.

Acadia is a dynamic landscape whose features change continually. The time frame can be quick and the magnitude of change small—as when a storm knocks down a stand of trees—or the transformation can be slower but more dramatic, such as when continental glaciation wears down a mountain. With every wave, every breath of wind, this process continues.

Creation of this extraordinary landscape began about 500 million years ago, when molten rock buried miles beneath the earth's surface began squeezing upward into fractures in the overlying strata. The eruption cooled partway to the surface and expanded, creating a huge dome of pink, coarse granite. Two-hundred million years of erosion wore away the surface layers overlying this dome, and a continuous east-west granite ridge called the Mount Desert Range lay revealed.

Then, about 20,000 years ago, the last of nine great continental glaciers advanced from Canada. The massive ice sheet—over a mile thick—traveled across the landscape scraping and gouging and tearing until it rammed into the Mount Desert Range lying directly across its path.

Voices in the Forest

These islands are so resilient. Their durability truly impresses me. For generations they were used hard—for quarries, timber, pasture—and left a wasteland. Today the islands are more forested than at any time in the last 300 years, and each is a wild world all its own. How humbling! We can almost wreck a place that will in the end outlast us. These islands are fragile as mountaintops, enduring as granite, mutable as the sand. There's so much going on here, where the rocky shoreline meets the sea, so much vitality. This is where the action is, where you can absolutely feel Nature's regenerative and transformational power.

ANNIE GETCHELL, *Maine-based writer, sea kayaker, and television host.*

The glacier stalled, but not for long. The force of billions of tons of flowing ice eventually won out, and the glacier overwhelmed the Mount Desert Range. Cutting and chiseling, the glacier crept up and over the pink granite ridge. The glacier then accelerated as it flowed down the face of the range toward the sea, cracking giant stone blocks from the mountain and carving the sheer cliffs along the ocean front.

When the glacier melted, approximately 13,000 years ago, the landscape left behind was drastically changed. The unbroken ridge of the Mount Desert Range was carved into a series of north-south ridges separated by wide U-shaped valleys. Some of the troughs and vales filled with water to become freshwater lakes and ponds. Others filled with seawater and became arms of the ocean. And as the ice sheet withdrew, giant boulders, called glacial erratics, were strewn about the landscape. Some ended up in improbable positions perched on the sides of mountains. When the ice cap melted the sea rose dramatically, flooding the continental shelf and drowning the valleys and hills, etching the meandering shoreline and myriad islands characteristic of the Maine coast today.

THE RUSTICATORS

Indigenous people may well have been witness at the close of the ice age—radiocarbon dating shows that Native Americans were living in the Northeast as many as 12,000 years ago and perhaps much longer. But because of Acadia's cool, moist, artifact-destroying climate, it may be impossible to pinpoint the earliest time of human occupation. However, shell piles prove that the Abenaki, who lived well off the riches of both land and sea, were present at least 6,000 years ago.

In 1613, not long after Champlain passed through, a group of French Jesuits established a mission on Fernald Point at the entrance to Somes Sound. But the dream of a French Acadia was dashed forever when a British warship commanded by Captain Samuel Argall—the same pirate who had abducted Pocahontas and carried her off to Jamestown—appeared out of the mist one spring morning and burned the mission to the ground. Argall took the survivors captive, selling some into slavery and casting the remainder adrift at sea. The incident was the opening salvo in the French and Indian Wars: a century and a half of brutal conflict between the two European powers for dominion in eastern North America.

The fleur-de-lis of France fluttered briefly once again over Acadia in 1688 when a young nobleman, Sieur Antonine de la Mothe Cadillac, attempted to establish an estate on Mount Desert Island. After a brief stay, Cadillac moved west to the Great Lakes, gaining fame as the founder of Detroit. Today, both Acadia's highest peak and Detroit's premier luxury car bear his name.

With the close of hostilities and the expulsion of France from eastern North America in the 1760s, the Maine coast was opened to English, and later American, settlement. By the early nineteenth century a prosperous farming, fishing, lumbering, and shipbuilding economy was well established on Mount Desert Island. These resource-based occupations still provide a way of life for some islanders.

For most, however, the pastoral existence vanished forever when the island was again "discovered," this time by Thomas Cole, Frederick Church, and the Hudson River School of painters in the mid-1800s. Their images of unspoiled natural beauty lured wealthy Boston and New York urbanites seeking relief from the oppressive heat of summer in the city.

They came by the thousands, these "rusticators," as they were called, boarding with local families and shifting the local economy to tourism. In 1872 Mount Desert Island bypassed even rival Newport when *Harper's* magazine named Eden (renamed Bar Harbor in 1919) the nation's most fashionable vacation spot.

During the Gilded Age many of the country's richest families—Vanderbilts, Rockefellers, Morgans, and Astors—built extravagant summer homes on the island. In keeping with the vacation atmosphere, they euphemistically referred to their elegant, fully staffed, fifty-room mansions as "cottages."

But the lavish parties and general gaiety of the times did not hide the fact that the island's natural beauty was being compromised by unfettered growth

After a day of sea kayaking, Mary Gorman stretches her legs on a fogbound, rocky island of the Maine coast.

OVERLEAF:
Otter Cliffs, Acadia National Park, Maine, at sunrise.

Dan Berns casts a line for breakfast from his island campsite at sunrise.

OPPOSITE:
Pink, glacier-scarred granite ledges lead to the summit of Cadillac Mountain in Acadia National Park.

and development. Several wealthy summer visitors, including Boston million-aire George Dorr, Harvard President Charles Eliot, and industrialist John D. Rockefeller Jr. joined in an effort to preserve the island's natural character.

These wealthy benefactors acquired and turned over to the public a patchwork of some six-thousand acres of coast, lakes, mountains, and forest. In 1916 their gift was dedicated as Sieur Des Monts National Monument. Later, this land formed the heart of the first national park east of the Mississippi River when Sieur Des Monts was rededicated as Lafayette National Park in 1919. Ten years later the park was renamed Acadia, which today totals some forty-thousand magnificent acres.

In 1949 a devastating forest fire swept Mount Desert Island, scorching eighteen-thousand acres over a two-week period. The fire changed the natural landscape by opening large clearings in the uniformly thick spruce-fir forest that had covered the island. Light-loving trees such as birch and aspen quickly colonized the gaps in the forest, adding color and contrast to the scene while providing browse for increased populations of white-tailed deer, beaver, and other hardwood forest dwellers. But by devouring many of the elegant Gilded Age mansions and hotels, the blaze effectively ended the era of opulence and cleared the way for a new social environment.

AT THE END OF THE TAILPIPE

Acadia has changed considerably over the years, and park managers cope with growing problems. As one of the country's most popular preserves, the park currently hosts some three million visitors annually, and at times the crowds seem overwhelming. The number of park visitors doubles every twenty years, and conservationists warn that Acadia is being "loved to death." They suggest that the very qualities people come here from around the world to enjoy—the natural beauty, the solace of the open spaces—are being degraded through sheer overuse.

A sunset over the Gulf of Maine, downeast Maine coast.

Other problems bedeviling managers have sources beyond the park's jurisdiction. Situated "at the end of the tailpipe" downwind from the rest of the country, Acadia is plagued by air pollution with origins hundreds of miles away in the Midwest. Perhaps most pressing is the virtually unregulated urban sprawl on Route 3, the park access road south of Ellsworth. This road leading to one of America's crown jewels is a ghastly concrete and glass gauntlet visitors must endure before they are allowed to enter the refuge of Acadia. The thoughtless development conflicts starkly with the natural beauty of the region, and it isolates Acadia as a wild island surrounded by cheap commercial expansion.

But Acadia's continued popularity attests to the fact that all is not yet lost. The park offers something for just about everyone, including some of the best and most diverse outdoor recreational opportunities in the United States. More than one hundred miles of maintained and marked trails provide a matchless network of mountain, forest, lakeshore, and ocean paths. The trails run the gamut from easy beach walking to strenuous all-day affairs climbing up precipitous cliffs and over bare granite summits. On clear days, paths such as the Western Head Trail on Isle au Haut, which offers spectacular views of the sea from high oceanside cliffs, present hiking opportunities that are unique in the United States.

In the early years of this century John D. Rockefeller built a system of carriage paths on Mount Desert Island that he placed strictly off limits to automobile travel. Rockefeller considered automobiles to be "infernal machines," and he felt the narrow, windy gravel paths provided a way to enjoy the magnificent scenery of Acadia without compromising the environment. Now restored, Rockefeller's legacy consists of a fifty-seven-mile-long network of maintained tracks winding through the eastern side of Mount Desert Island. Still barred to automobiles, the paths are perfect for walking, skiing, horseback riding, and mountain biking. They are a wonderful and fitting way to explore the park and enjoy the ocean views, interior lakes, forests, mountains, and waterfalls.

REFUGE

Every generation seems to rediscover Acadia, and today rock climbers are pioneering routes on the park's cliffs. Here, at the very edge of the crashing sea, clean, pink granite walls rise directly above the swells. Although not particularly long, the routes at Otter Cliffs are of exceptional quality, and the special character and unique ambiance of the seaside setting make this a truly unforgettable climbing venue.

The splendid view from the water has not diminished since Champlain's day, and growing numbers of people are discovering that the sea kayak is the vessel perhaps best suited for exploring these islands, bays, inlets, and the nearby coast. This is also fitting, for in keeping with the transformation of Acadia from private playground of rusticators to refuge for ordinary people, the pleasures of coasting here are no longer the sole province of the yacht set. In a sea kayak you can circumnavigate Mount Desert Island or Isle au Haut, paddle out to the Porcupine Islands off Bar Harbor, or sneak off to some deserted shelf of rock in Merchant Row near Deer Isle.

On my most recent trip to Acadia and the islands near Isle au Haut, I felt like Champlain might have when a cold wave crashed across my deck and pummeled me in the chest. I felt as though I were paddling through cotton gauze, for I couldn't see the islands in the mist. Watching my compass closely, factoring in the drift of the tide and the push of the breeze, I stuck to a course and was somewhat astonished when a couple of hours later the bow of my kayak nearly split the little fog-shrouded island I was aiming for.

Setting up my tent, watching the mist curl through the dark trees, I felt like an explorer finding my way through the unknown. Settling down on a smooth granite shelf with a hot drink, rubbing muscles tired from paddling for many miles, I felt completely self-sufficient and quite content. Everything I needed was stored in the watertight bulkheads of my kayak: food, clothing, shelter, and fresh water for days. I could go anywhere. I shared the same sense of freedom and discovery with all those who had paddled and sailed here before.

In the morning the sun rose from the sea like a molten rock, and a pod of porpoises swam across the glowing tide. The silhouette of their arched backs formed black crescent shapes on the water, and their dorsal fins rose and fell with a graceful rhythm.

OPPOSITE:

A seak kayaker paddles the shoreline of an island in Merchant Row near Acadia National Park.

DOWN THE FALL LINE

Six inches of fresh snow carpet the slopes at Killington, Vermont, and the air is thick with flying flakes, reducing visibility in the tight trees to only a few yards. I'm down under the canopy skiing fast, turning quickly where the terrain allows. As a dyed-in-the-wool Yankee bark eater, I know that in the pucker brush you don't ski with a rigid plan. You keep the boards pointed down the fall line, let your skills and instincts take over, and just react.

Since it's Wednesday and the weekend crowds are nowhere in sight, there's no question of slowing down. Like a hound dog chasing a rabbit hell-bent for his hidey-hole I tear through the grove, shooting through tight gaps and threading needle's-eye passageways. Zigging and zagging, dodging stumps and knocking snow off spruce boughs, I have no idea where I am or where I'm going. I'm just trying to keep Chris Mangini's elusive blue parka in sight before he drops over a lip and disappears again.

For more than twenty years, an informal nonorganization called the Tasmanian Telemarkers has rallied at the K-1 gondola at Killington. "I did the math last night," says Mangini. "We've been doing this for over 365 Wednesdays. That's a year of Wednesdays!"

We pop into an open glade and Mangini slides to a stop. Grinning like a thief who just pulled off the biggest heist of his career, he leans back and bellows "Ah-Ooooo!" to the treetops, then smiles as the sound echoes through the glade. It's the Tasmanian Telemarker rallying cry, the call of the pack, an expression of pure joy. Soon some twenty other free-heel skiers appear out of the trees. Men and women ranging from their mid-twenties to mid-fifties, they yammer about the snow, the trees, the skiing.

Trailing a billowing cloud, a skier blasts through a foot of cold, fresh powder.

Voices in the Forest

Sliding down snow-covered mountains powered by gravity has been a source of joy and inspiration for folks up here for generations. Skiing is a cherished tradition all across the region. It's a sport, but it's also a way of life, a part of the culture. And while we're out enjoying the mountains, we're also providing a healthy and environmentally sound economic base for the North Country. 🍂

TED AUSTIN, *general manager, Cranmore Mountain Resort.*

Mangini listens to the banter for a moment, and then asks, "Okay, how many telemarkers does it take to screw in a lightbulb? Five. One to screw in the bulb and four to talk about how good the turns were!" He laughs at his joke, yells, "Ah-ooo!" again, and then takes off. And once more I'm chasing a contrail shimmering in the frosty air.

The Tasmanians began skiing at Killington in the late 1970s, teaching themselves the lost art of free-heel telemark skiing by experimenting with cross-country equipment on the Alpine slopes. "Back then the tele skis we had were skinny little sticks with no side cut," says Peter Kavouksorian, an original Tasmanian from Rutland. "They were essentially javelins. They just wouldn't turn. If you wanted to change directions you literally had to do jump turns."

Despite the primitive gear, Peter, his wife, JoAnn, and several other pioneering free-heel skiers began competing in the weekly races held at Killington. Searching for a whimsical team name to reflect their odd skiing style, they called themselves the Tasmanian Telemarkers. Soon other local central Vermont skiers—Murray and Patty McGrath, John Tidd, Chris Mangini, Mark Heckman, John McGurk, Pam Darrow, and others—cast aside their Alpine gear and began showing up to race with skinny skis. It didn't take long for them to realize that what brought them together wasn't competition, but the fun and challenge of learning together what was then considered an avant-garde form of skiing.

But rather than revolutionaries on the cutting edge, the Tasmanians were actually throwbacks to an earlier era and heirs to a rich tradition. Telemark skiing is actually the original form of controlled, purposeful downhill skiing (as opposed to merely straight-running down hills without steering). The skill was invented in the Telemark region of Norway by a farmer named Sondre Norheim, who unveiled his radical turning technique in 1868. The method Norheim invented to steer his skis—dropping into a crouch with one ski forward and one ski back—quickly became known throughout Norway as the "Telemark turn."

FIRST TRACKS IN THE NORTH COUNTRY

It wasn't long after Norheim startled his countrymen with his breakthrough technique that the snowbound residents of the Great Northern Forest took up skiing for fun and transport. Norwegian loggers established the country's first ski club in Berlin, New Hampshire, in 1882, and by the turn of the century, the sport's popularity was firmly established among local residents and visitors alike. Winter—once seen as a season to endure with stoicism, a bottle of hooch, and most likely a virulent case of cabin fever—became the most anticipated time of year for many as people eagerly took to sliding down the bright snowy slopes on skis.

In the first decades of the twentieth century, prior to the advent of the mechanical ski lift, skiers were typically equally adept at going uphill, downhill, cross-country, and even jumping. This was long before the age of specialization, so they did it all with the same pair of stout hickory skis. And because skiers had to earn their turns by climbing up whatever they wished to ski down, their heels were not locked down but instead were free to lift on the ascent.

During the 1930s, the Civilian Conservation Corps built a lasting legacy and added to the region's rich skiing heritage when the men cut dozens of recreational downhill ski trails in the mountainous North Country. Many of those challenging wilderness trails— the Nose Dive, Teardrop, and Bruce trails in Vermont; the Richard Taft, Wildcat, and Gulf of Slides trails in New Hampshire, among many others—are still used by backcountry telemark skiers today.

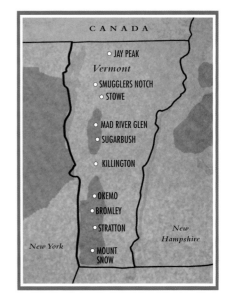

More than a century after those wool-clad loggers took to the slopes around Berlin, America's skiing heritage is deeply rooted in the mountains of northern New England and upstate New York. The first slalom ski race in the United States was held at Dartmouth College in New Hampshire in 1923, and the first downhill ski race in the country was held on New Hampshire's Mount Moosilauke in 1927. The nation's first ski school opened in Sugar Hill, New Hampshire, in 1929, and the first Winter Olympics (with cross-country skiing and ski jumping events only) hosted by the United States were held in the Adirondacks in Lake Placid, New York, in 1932. The first giant slalom ski race ever held in the United States took place in Tuckerman Ravine, on New Hampshire's Mount Washington, in 1937.

And finally, in the spirit of Yankee ingenuity, Yankee contrariness, and Yankee love of winter, the tradition-snubbing and wildly popular snowboard was invented here in these well-wooded hills and presented to the world in 1977 by Vermont's own Jake Burton Carpenter.

With such a rich heritage, it should be no surprise that the region has produced an impressive number of Olympic skiers (and snowboard riders). New Hampshire, where skiing is the official state sport, has sent athletes to every Winter Olympics since 1942, when downhill skiing was first introduced to the Olympic Games. Not to be outdone of course, neighboring Vermont has sent more skiers to the Olympics than any other state in the country.

FREE RIDE

Something revolutionary happened to the culture and economy of the North Country on January 18, 1934, in Woodstock, Vermont. On that day Robert Bourdon became the first skier in the country to be pulled to the top of a hill by a rope tow. Consisting of an 1,800-foot-long loop of rope running over a series of pulleys set on posts, the rope tow was powered by a Model-T Ford. In about a minute, the tow hauled a skier up the 900 foot slope of Clinton Gilbert's farm pasture, and it could pull as many as five skiers at once! For the first time ever skiers could simply ride to the summit, and they could enjoy as many downhill runs in the same day as they wished—just as long as they were willing to pay the $1 a day fee to use the tow. Suddenly, skiing was no longer just a backcountry pastime. People no longer needed to climb, and most folks were only too happy to trade in their do-it-all free-heel skis for a pair of new metal-edged skis mounted with fixed heel bindings. Almost overnight skiing became a predominantly downhill sport.

Within a short time almost every town in the region with a hill had a rope tow, and some of these community ski hills are still in operation. However, not satisfied with the rope tow's limited speed and capacity, crafty Yankees developed new and faster ways to get people to the mountain summits. In 1938 the country's first aerial tramway was opened on Cannon Mountain in New

Hampshire, chairlifts began replacing surface tows, and the era of the modern destination ski resort began.

In the years after World War II what became known as "the ski industry" became a major economic force in the North Country. New ski areas were built, others expanded, and snowmaking systems were invented and installed to provide excellent conditions even when nature didn't cooperate. By the mid-1960s there were hundreds of small, medium, and large ski slopes throughout the region—Vermont alone boasted more than eighty ski areas in 1966.

Though the total number of ski areas in the North Country has declined since the mid-sixties (the New England Lost Ski Area Project—www.nelsap.org—lists 460 once operational but now closed areas!). The eighty or so survivors have either found a niche or merged and expanded into some of the most successful resorts in the country. And the major resorts in the North Country are the equals of any in North America. Vermont, New Hampshire, and Maine currently have a combined fourteen ski areas with vertical drops of two thousand feet or more, the same number as Colorado, and six more than Utah. And though the quality of the snow is sometimes questioned by those "from away," it does fall in large quantities, with most of the major resorts averaging more than twenty feet of snow annually. Jay Peak in northern Vermont, home of the infamous Jay Cloud that seems to spew powder on a nonstop basis all winter long, averages about thirty feet of snow annually—more than Vail or Aspen.

Skiing's impact on the North Country's economy is enormous. New Hampshire alone hosts more than 2.6 million skier visits each year. According to state figures, skiing pumps more than half a billion dollars into the New Hampshire economy annually.

For the first time ever, skiers could simply ride to the summit—if they were willing to pay $1 a day.

BALANCING ACT

Of course, not everyone is completely thrilled with the mergers, acquisitions, and expansions that have rocked the ski industry in recent years, and the ski industry has its share of detractors in the environmental community. These critics point out that, whereas a few decades ago most ski areas were just that —places to ski—the financial realities of the modern ski industry require the creation of what one ski resort master plan calls "year-round vertically integrated resorts," or entertainment complexes based upon the Disney World and Las Vegas models in the middle of pristine wildlands. No longer just a place to catch a lift to the top of the slopes, these multifaceted recreation centers are very sophisticated, high-risk businesses requiring long-term capital investments in new lifts, expanded snowmaking systems, enhanced base facilities, luxury hotels and condominiums, and four-season recreational facilities calculated to attract ever larger numbers of people.

Telemark skier Jamie Corsiglia enjoys four feet of fresh powder at Sugarbush, Vermont, the day after a major nor'easter.

When operated in an environmentally sensitive manner, ski resorts can minimize their impacts on the landscape. However, a ski resort is an intensive use of the land, and significant environmental impacts caused by ski resorts can include deforestation, soil erosion, destruction of critical wildlife habitat, depletion of stream flows, damage to sensitive wetlands, increased vehicle traffic, urban congestion, and the general degradation of the peace, quiet, and beauty of natural settings.

Surveys regularly demonstrate that skiers are a very environmentally inclined group and are more likely than the average person to belong to an environmental organization or to vote based upon a candidate's environmental positions. But skier-environmentalists are sometimes caught in a dilemma between enjoying their sport and feeling the need to protect the environment from resort managers who seek to maximize profits at the expense of the pristine wildlands—the very thing that attracts visitors in the first place.

Voices in the Forest

The wood products industry will never sustain this region like it did....We should try to strengthen what is working, which at the moment is skiing.... People refer to the "good old days"—formerly known as "these trying times." The people whose ancestors lived here aren't saying "'leave things alone." I haven't heard anyone whose house is falling down and whose job closed at the mill saying "Let's preserve this."

LES OTTEN, *developer and former owner of Killington, Sunday River, and other American Ski Company Resorts.*

"We have met the enemy, and once again, it is us," a dedicated environmentalist who is also an avid skier told me. He went on to say that he was far from being alone in his predicament, but that it was hard for him and for other skier-environmentalists to blame the ski industry for any wrongdoings "because that means accepting that we are a part of the problem."

Responding to both internal and external pressure, the National Ski Area Association, the trade organization for 332 alpine ski resorts nationwide, worked with the United States Forest Service, the Environmental Protection Agency, the Conservation Law Foundation, and other organizations to develop and implement the Environmental Charter for Ski Areas. The charter contains a set of voluntary principles for protecting the environment, and it provides a frame work for resorts across the country to implement best practices, assess environmental performances, and set goals for improvement. Addressing all aspects of resort operation, including planning and design, water and energy use, habitat and forest management, and waste management, the charter formalizes the industry's commitment to environmental sustainability and stewardship.

But whereas some North Country resorts embraced growth and development in recent decades, others barred the door to modern development and commercialization. In time-honored and tradition-bound Yankee fashion, these areas—and the skiers who frequent them—pride themselves on going about their business as generations did before them. When the American Ski Company floated the idea of perhaps replacing the slow, widely spaced Castle Rock double chair at Sugarbush with a faster, higher-capacity lift, the company literally faced a rebellion from skiers who rightly pointed out that adding skiers would destroy the quality and integrity of the quiet, private, woodsy

trail network. And in bold, even religious, defiance of anything new, Mad River Glen and its passionate skier-owners refuse to replace the main lift to the summit—a single-seat chair installed in 1949. These and other classic North Country ski areas—with their lovingly cut steep and narrow trails and hardwood glades—truly fit into the landscape as if they belong there.

The Northern Forest is the cradle of American skiing, with a rich heritage and strong traditions dating back to the 1800s.

LOOK AT THOSE OLD GUYS RIP!

Back on the slopes at Killington, I wonder if Sondre Norheim had any idea what he was starting when he took that first telemark turn on some wild, snow-covered pasture in Norway a century and a half ago. Could he have foreseen the perfectly groomed trails, or the Skyeship gondola whisking people to the top, or the towering snowmaking guns? One thing I'm sure of: he would

be deeply impressed by the skiing talent gathered here on these seven mountain peaks cut by ninety miles of trails and served by thirty-two high-speed lifts. For after twenty years, the Tasmanian Telemarkers finally have equipment to match their abilities.

Gone are the skinny double-camber misery sticks and the soft leather lace-up boots. Those have thankfully given way to super-fat, super-side cut skis powered by stiff four-buckle plastic boots. Gore-Tex has replaced wool, helmets have replaced hats, and a super-aggressive down-the-fall-line style of telemarking has replaced the graceful swooping turns of just a few years ago. It's quite a sight to watch a couple dozen Tasmanians ripping down the toughest slopes together with perfect grace and style, reaching back into the past to bring Norheim's turn into modern times. Alpine or free-heel, these are some of the best skiers I've ever seen. Halfway down bumped-up Superstar I pull over just to watch, and I overhear a couple of teenage snowboarders talking:

Facing down the fall line on a bright spring morning.

"Look at those old guys rip!"

"Yeah, do you think they're a team or something?"

As we ride the gondola back to the summit of Killington Peak, John Tidd, a former Professional Ski Instructors of America National Nordic Team member and an original Tasmanian, reminisces about how when he was a kid he used to earn lift passes on the once-and-future single chair at Mad River Glen, Vermont, by helping to boot-pack the slopes back in the days before grooming equipment.

"But that's what skiing is really all about," he says. "Working together, playing together, and being outdoors together in the snow and fresh air."

And that, he explains, is the secret to the Tasmanians' continuity as they head into their third decade. "We're a family," he says. "A lot of us have been skiing together for a long time, and we've kind of grown up together. But everyone is welcome to come out and play. In skiing, it doesn't take long for a fresh face to become an old friend. That's why on Wednesdays we always meet at the gondola at ten and in the base lodge at one—to pick up newcomers or latecomers." Then he adds, "After a couple of runs, most people pretty much know whether or not they want to hang with us."

At the end of the day, I'm still hanging—and loving it. Run after scorching run, the group generates its own energy, a power source that drives us long after our own personal batteries have been depleted. When the lifts close I feel surprisingly fresh and exhilarated.

Down on the Killington access road there's a tavern that's been laying out an après-ski spread for the Tasmanians for years. We rendezvous there for a cold draft and a hot meal, relax in front of the snapping fire, and relive the day's spills and thrills in the North Country snows. As I tear myself away, I hear voices call out, "See you next Wednesday!"

I'll be there.

Powder snow explodes as a skier rips through a Northern Forest glade on a sparkling winter day.

A PERFECT WILDERNESS

❧

The ducks seem unsettled. Their agitated prattle carries sharply across the water as they fuss among themselves, trying to get it together. It's that time of year, autumn—the beginning and the end of everything—a season tinged with both hope and regret. A chill is in the air, the birds have their down coats on, and the wanderlust is upon them. For the ducks, these false starts are a tiresome but necessary part of the process. The next storm will probably send them on their way.

We slip the green canoe into the black waters of Cranberry Lake in New York's Adirondack Park, clove-hitch the bow painter to a maple sapling, then hike through the woods to get the gear. Staggering back down the trail under a couple of heavy canvas Duluth packs, I dump the load by the put-in. There isn't a breath of wind to mar the lake's mirror surface. The cool, early-morning air is sharp in the nostrils, fir scented, and so pure I just relax for a moment and quaff it like spring water.

Out on the lake, the raft of mallards abruptly takes flight. Dozens of wings and webbed feet slap the smooth surface in an arrhythmic percussion that swells like applause to a ragged crescendo. The flock lifts, makes a wide, wavering circle above the low Adirondack hills, then splashes back down just as suddenly, scant yards from where it took off only moments before.

I store a mesh decoy bag amidships, then place my shotgun securely in the bow. I'm glad to see the birds are still here. It's been a long time since I hunted ducks, a long time since I hunted at all, for that matter. Over the years other pursuits intruded and I discovered that I had phased myself out of hunting.

Dan Berns sets out duck decoys. Ringed by the fiery reflection of late-autumn hardwood forests, the lake stretches off the range of vision.

When my friend Dan called and suggested this trip to the Adirondacks, I realized how much I missed it, and I decided to phase myself back in.

We load the rest of the gear and shove off. My hands find their accustomed places on the shaft of my traditional Maine Guide paddle. I notice that my palms have polished the blond ash to a shiny gloss. I take a stroke, then another. Black water gurgles behind the sweep of the hand-shaped blade. The canoe slips forward. Soon we're gliding smoothly across the reflected heavens, through an armada of puffy white clouds. We pass the tip of a rocky point, and the horizon unfolds in all directions as we enter the main body of Cranberry Lake.

LAND OF THE BARK EATERS

Ringed by the fiery reflection of late-autumn hardwood forests, the lake stretches off to the north beyond the range of vision. In that sweep of distance there isn't another boat, nor can I detect even a small break in the trees framing the shoreline. This is a big blank spot on the map, and we've got the one essential freedom—time—to lose ourselves in it. We'll spend the next week or so exploring this wild and little-visited part of the park.

The Adirondacks have always been a place apart. Even the Mohawks found conditions here too harsh for permanent settlement—although they used the land seasonally for hunting and fishing for at least two thousand years. "Adirondack" means "bark eater" in Iroquois and the Mohawks used it to taunt their ancient foes, the Abenaki. The insult implied that the Abenaki were such awful hunters they had to take bites out of trees.

To European settlers, the Adirondacks were initially worthless. Scattered settlements in the fertile Champlain Valley and around the edges of the mountains sprouted in the late 1700s, but no one was interested in the interior. Free Adirondack land was offered to Revolutionary War veterans, but there were few takers, and the rugged mountains were ignored. So ignored, for example, that the source of the Nile—deep in the equatorial jungles of Africa—was actually discovered before the birthplace of the Hudson was discovered, at Lake Tear of the Clouds high upon the great peak the Mohawks called "The Cloudsplitter"—now known as Mount Marcy. The Adirondack region remained all but unknown until the 1830s, some three decades after Lewis and Clark went west, when an official exploration party was finally dispatched.

Eventually profit-hungry entrepreneurs realized the value of the resource-

rich Adirondacks. By the late 1800s, more than five million acres of virgin forest had been clear-cut, and wildfires burned much of what hadn't been cut over.
Fearing that deforestation, followed by erosion and evaporation, would damage
the Hudson River for industry and commerce downstream, the New York legislature began buying land to protect Adirondack watersheds. In 1894 these
lands were placed in a public reserve to be "forever kept as wild forest."

Saved by the people of New York for essentially ecological purposes some
seventy-five years before the words "environmental movement" entered the
lexicon, today the Adirondack Park is a vast green island of anonymous
forested hills, spruce bogs, wetlands, and tangled hardwood thickets—the old, eternal wilderness—precisely
the kind of fish- and game-rich lands that have been
cut, drained, built up, and paved over just about everywhere else. At six million acres the Adirondack Park is
larger than Yellowstone, Glacier, Yosemite, Olympic, and
Grand Canyon National Parks combined.

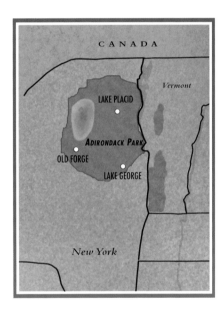

Roughly 90 percent of all protected wilderness east
of the Mississippi and north of the Mason-Dixon Line
lies in the Adirondack Park, as do 2,800 ponds and lakes,
1,500 miles of rivers, and 30,000 miles of brooks and
streams. There are also 100 peaks topping 3,000 feet, with
46 over 4,000 feet. Then there are some 2,000 miles of
hiking trails, "some going to places so remote you
wouldn't see a soul back there if you spent all summer,"
according to Adirondack conservationist Dick Beamish.

In terms of its sheer size, diversity of terrain, reserves of plant and animal
life, and quality of recreational opportunities, the Adirondack Park is in every
sense a national park—except for the fact that 130,000 permanent residents
and 200,000 seasonal residents live within its boundaries.

THE COST OF DEVELOPMENT

For well over a century, people have lived, worked, and owned homes and businesses in this checkerboard of public and private property. Unlike national parks
and federally designated wilderness areas, the Adirondack Park is wilderness
interwoven with human settlement. Roughly 40 percent of the park is in public

Sunset on an Adirondack lake, New York.

ownership, "forever wild" under the state constitution. The rest is private—timberland, developer-owned vacation land, houses, and small hamlets. Every year as many as 1,000 new homes are built in the Adirondacks despite a complicated system of regional planning.

In 1967 the Adirondack Northway, a superhighway making the park accessible to the urban centers downstate, was completed. Almost immediately a second-home boom was ignited. Seemingly overnight, vacation bungalows sprouted like mushrooms. In 1971, when it became clear that unregulated development threatened to destroy the open-space character of the park, the Adirondack Park Agency (APA) was created to oversee land use and zoning.

But before the APA could become an effective agency, politically powerful pro-development forces extracted a heavy price from state legislators. They demanded that the lakeshores be placed in a zoning category called

"moderate intensity use," meaning that cabins can be built cheek-to-jowl on every 1.3 acres of privately owned waterfront. In the backcountry away from the lakes, development was restricted to one building on every 42.7 acres, a policy that, instead of preserving vast areas of open space by clustering development, actually encourages the conversion of undeveloped lands into suburban sprawl.

The APA isn't able to do much to keep the park from becoming wilderness suburbia. Although the agency was given a broad mandate by the state legislature to regulate development, it was given almost no enforcement power, and only a handful of officers to review all building proposals in the six-million-acre park. Not surprisingly, a great deal of illegal building goes on—by some estimates only one-fifth of all development activities within the park boundaries are reviewed by the APA.

In the past few years, however, there has been widespread public and political support for conservation efforts in the Adirondacks. There is also a sense of urgency, a feeling that the time to obtain the last scattered wild parcels and put them in public ownership is running out.

"It's the best of times and the worst of times," Dick Beamish told me when I visited him at his cabin near Lake Clear. "Development continues to be a serious threat, especially to the lakeshores. On the other hand, in many ways the park is wilder than it was 100 years ago. The trees in the Forest Preserve haven't been cut in a hundred years! This is an old-growth forest factory!

"And you know," he continues, "there are places with higher mountains, or bigger forests, or more lakes and ponds, but there's no place where you have all these elements combined as we have them in the Adirondacks. This park is worth saving, and we've never had a better opportunity to do it than we have right now. If we can mobilize the support, we'll prevail."

THE ORIGINAL CONSERVATIONISTS

Dan peels off about sixty feet of fly line. There's a streamer tied to the sharp end. He's constitutionally unable to refrain from either hunting or fishing while on the move, a disorder he has no trouble accepting. "Look," he says, "as long as we're paddling we might as well troll."

We choose a course that passes several rocky islets. Nothing. Next we swing past the mouth of a small stream. Gliding by the inlet, I glance over my shoulder as the line goes taut. The rod slips against the deck plate, and Dan reaches for it with one hand while stowing his paddle with the other. A small but intense battle ensues as Dan and the fish pursue mutually exclusive goals. I stop paddling and watch as he deftly plays the fish, coaxes him close to the canoe, and then scoops him into the net.

It's a handsome brook trout, lean and firm, iridescent and splendidly mottled. The fish strikes me as the very embodiment of this watery autumn wilderness. We repeat the scene a couple of times, and before long we have enough fish for tonight's main course. With Dan there's little reason to pack a lot of extra food. Usually, the land and water provide everything he needs to make a meal. Paddling with more purpose now, we enter the long dark arm of Dead Creek Flow and find a camp for the night.

After breakfast the next morning we cache the canoe and the rods, hoist packs and guns, and take to the trail. Like my paddle, the Browning feels like it belongs in my hands. And when I work the forearm slide to jack the shells, the action makes a smooth, precise, and familiar sound that invests the day with an intense and undeniable gravity.

Voices in the Forest

There were many abuses of the land in the past. People were careless, and we had to change. But now the reaction has gone overboard. Look at the Adirondack Park. It was a noble undertaking at the time — the Forever Wild clause in the state constitution. But now you can't cut a stick of wood in it. The park is administered by a fairly elite group, and the people who live there never had much of a say. They don't have the numbers, they don't have the political clout, or the money. That's why there is such bitterness. The Adirondackers look at those trees and say, "Look at the wood rotting . . . and our kids have to go downstate to get a job flipping hamburgers.

STEVE MONGAN, *forester for Landvest.*

Hiking into the Five Ponds Wilderness, we skirt a handful of hidden lakes. From the summit of Cat Mountain we look out over a flaming mixed hardwood forest spread at our feet like a bed of hot coals stretching to the horizon. Back down in the lowlands we pick a meandering route around bogs and beaver flows and fragrant spruce thickets. We tramp across upland ridges thick with stands of beech trees shot through with golden sunlight and bursting with trembling yellow leaves.

It's a flawless day in perfect terrain for grouse, and we hike along slowly, listening for a flutter of wings or the sound of a distant drummer. I try to remember to look up now and then and scan the trees, not just the ground cover, because the birds love their high perches. Ahead and to the right a grouse drums with the sound of a lawnmower kicking to life. Dropping packs on the trail, we split up and begin stalking slowly and quietly, working the cover on separate transits, stopping frequently to look and listen.

Whirring wings break the silence from up the hill to my right. I spot the grouse rocketing overhead and fire. But the bird is so fast he's just a brown blur and I'm not even close. Sometime later Dan is successful, and we drop down off the long ridge with the seasonal, locally grown, organic fixings for another delicious dinner—indeed the definitive macrobiotic meal.

No thinking person heads off willy-nilly into the wilds in pursuit of his or her fellow creatures. So before I decided to carry a fly rod and a firearm on this journey, I reread an essay by Thomas McGuane tilted "The Heart of the Game." In it there is a passage that describes exactly how I feel right now:

"Nobody who loves to hunt feels absolutely hunky-dory when the quarry goes down. The remorse spins out almost before anything and the balancing act ends on one declination or another. I decided that unless I become a vegetarian, I'll get my meat by hunting for it. I feel absolutely unabashed by the arguments of other carnivores who get their meat in plastic with blue numbers on it. I've seen slaughterhouses, and anyway, as Sitting Bull said, when the buffalo are gone, we will hunt mice, for we are hunters and we want our freedom."

In the Adirondacks, all across the Northern Forest, and virtually everywhere else in rural America, active participation in the cycles of nature is still a very important part of life. For generations Americans have renewed their ties to the land in the most direct way through hunting, fishing, and gathering wild fruits, nuts, and vegetables. To do so successfully requires a profound understanding not only of the species sought but of the entire ecosystem as well.

Those who engage in these activities often develop deep personal connections to the source of bounty—the land. Many of America's greatest conservation leaders—Theodore Roosevelt, Frederick Law Olmstead, John James Audubon, George Perkins Marsh, Sigurd Olson, Henry David Thoreau, Aldo Leopold, Olaus Murie, Bob Marshall, and Jimmy Carter among them—were hunters and anglers. Leopold's *A Sand County Almanac* is perhaps America's most popular and celebrated conservation manifesto, so it might come as a surprise that Leopold is also widely considered the father of modern game management. And while Thoreau's *Walden* celebrates living simply in harmony with nature, he found his models for living in the stalwart, practical people who worked outdoors. In *Walden* Thoreau wrote:

> Fishermen, hunters, woodchoppers, and others, spending their lives in the fields and woods, in a particular sense a part of nature, are often in a more favorable mood for observing her, in the intervals of their pursuits, than philosophers or poets even, who approach her with expectation. She is not afraid to exhibit herself to them. The traveler on the prairie is naturally a hunter, on the headwaters of the Missouri and Columbia a trapper, and at the falls of St. Mary a fisherman. He who is only a traveler learns things at second-hand and by the halves, and is poor authority.

The country's rapidly growing population has become ever more urban and suburban since Thoreau was writing in the 1850s, and today conservation-minded men and women who hunt and fish are no longer widely considered role models. On the contrary, they increasingly find themselves under attack. All across America's sprawling urban and suburban landscapes it has become generally acceptable to vilify hunters as "gun nuts" and "drunks who shoot at anything that moves."

WHERE IS THE RECOGNITION?

Unfortunately for the environment, these attitudes alienate millions of hunters who care deeply about the land. After all, perhaps better than anyone hunters understand that abundant wildlife populations require habitat—a healthy base of wild and open land.

"We've created a huge socioeconomic divide," David Getchell, a Camden, Maine, writer, filmmaker, and conservationist told me. "Even though they are often the best conservationists, we have pushed the hunters, the anglers, and the trappers straight into the hands of pro development, reactionary conservative politicians. The hunters are a surprisingly conservation-oriented group with a much better connection to the land than the average recreationalist. But if you were in their shoes, if you were constantly accused of moral and intellectual incapacity by suburban environmentalists, what would you do when it came time to go to the polls?"

John Harrigan, a newspaper publisher, conservationist, and hunter in Coos County, New Hampshire, agrees. Speaking of the great gulf between down-state and out-of-state suburbanites and his neighbors, he says, "Those people are so out-of-step with rural America it's frightening. There is no tolerance anymore. Of course, as with any large group there are exceptions, and not all hunters make us proud. But for more than a century the vast majority of hunters have been at the forefront of the land protection movement. Where is the recognition for all they have accomplished?"

Where indeed? Each year hunters and anglers pour more money directly into land and wildlife conservation than any other sector of American society. Waterfowl hunters finance the National Wildlife Refuge System through the Federal Duck Stamp Program (FDSP). For every Federal Duck Stamp sold, one-tenth of an acre of wetlands is saved forever from development. So far, the FDSP has contributed to the permanent preservation of 4.16 million acres of habitat for wetland species.

> ## Voices in the Forest
>
> *When we lived in Canaan, Vermont, there were months when we depended upon hunting, fishing, and gathering to eat. We would hike an hour to get brook trout. But we're seeing the end of hunting as we know it. This is strange stuff. I hunt and fish, but I find myself doing it less and less—it's hard to get away without being harassed. The enmity between groups is enormous.*
>
> E. ANNIE PROULX, *Pulitzer Prize winning author of* The Shipping News.

But that's just the beginning. State hunting and fishing licenses generate millions more dollars annually for wildlife habitat preservation and restoration projects all across the country. The Federal Aid in Wildlife Restoration and Sport Fishing Act, commonly known as the Pittman-Robertson Act (a federal excise tax on hunting equipment and ammunition), currently raises nearly $200 million annually for habitat restoration and wildlife research. The Wallop-Breaux amendment (a Federal excise tax on sportfishing equipment) currently raises yet another $240 million each year for lake and stream restoration, research, and education.

Those are merely the dollars every hunter and angler must spend, voluntarily or not, to purchase licenses and gear. But the conservation story doesn't end there. Through membership in private organizations, hunters and anglers have been working quietly but effectively for decades to protect wild land from development and to enhance wildlife populations. According to research by Ted Kerasote, nature writer and editor of the Pew Wilderness Center's *Return of the Wild,* the numbers are impressive. He found that since 1937 the members of Ducks Unlimited have raised and spent $1.4 billion to preserve ten million acres of wetlands, an area more than twice the size of the state of New Jersey. The members of the Rocky Mountain Elk Foundation have anted up $154 million to purchase three million acres, lands equivalent to an area more than eight times the size of Bryce Canyon National Park.

The National Wild Turkey Federation doesn't make headlines, but its members have raised $120 million and saved 2.2 million acres, an area the size of Yellowstone National Park. A little group of 90,000 members called Pheasants Forever may not be well-known, but its members have raised some $70 million and preserved two million acres for wildlife—a land area roughly twice the size of Glacier National Park. And many more millions of acres have been saved by the members of other hunter and angler organizations, including the Ruffed Grouse Society, Trout Unlimited, the Isaac Walton League, and Quail Unlimited, among others.

Protecting many of the unique qualities of the Great Northern Forest may come down in part to a long, difficult campaign of purchasing the land acre by acre from willing sellers. In that case conservationists who neither hunt nor fish will do well to follow the example of, and join ranks with, the nation's seventeen million hunters and sixty million anglers who share their long-term goals and who have been protecting land and wildlife for over a century. Such an alliance would create an invincible, politically centrist coalition for the defense of wild places.

THE BOB

The water is cold and murky and up to our knees. Hiking along the Oswegatchie River, we're sloshing through a pond where the map insists there's a trail. But the trail is long gone, drowned by some industrious beaver clan. The path has probably been flooded for years. But it's so far back in the bush, the trail crews have no doubt forgotten it ever existed.

Fine. Such back-of-beyond wilds may not blow you away with their transparent beauty. But they do offer something equally important: solitude. There's simply no reason for most people to go there. Accordingly, I find myself increasingly drawn to the blackfly-bitten, blown-down, neglected wilds, keeping company with the surly black bear, the furtive wood duck, and a few iconoclastic, beaver-flow-dwelling brook trout.

In the summer of 1922, a young man named Bob Marshall attended the New York State College of Forestry's base camp not far from Cranberry Lake. During his free time and on weekends, the tireless Marshall, who loved to put twenty or thirty miles under his boots between sunup and sundown, slung on a backpack and took to the surrounding woods and streams. Driven by an irrepressible need to explore, he assessed the country and inventoried all the ponds, rivers, and streams from Cranberry Lake south all the way to the Beaver River.

He never forgot what he saw on those long rambles. Later, as a division chief in the U.S. Forest Service, Marshall compiled a record of roadless areas in the United States of 300,000 acres or more. His list included forty-eight wild places not yet "transformed to asphalt," as he put it, places big enough to travel in for two weeks without crossing your own tracks. He hoped to protect these lands in a wilderness preservation system, and the enormous Cranberry Lake–Beaver River country was on his list. Due to its remoteness and to the fact that roughly half of the land is publicly owned, the country is remarkably unchanged since Marshall took its measure eight decades ago. Today, many conservationists would like to see it protected as The Bob Marshall Great Wilderness, or simply "The Bob."

And their dream is now within reach. Key large private landholdings within "The Bob" have come up for sale in recent years, and many of these have been protected through new conservation partnerships employing a wide range of innovative conservation tools. Teaming with organizations such as The Nature Conservancy and the Conservation Fund, Governor Pataki and New York State have led the way in protecting important pieces within "The Bob" by purchasing lands and/or conservation easements in critical wild areas. By 2002 these acquisitions totaled nearly 200,000 acres.

A hunter takes aim at a flight of mallards. An alliance of hunters and fishermen with conservationists who neither hunt nor fish would create an invincible, politically centrist coalition for the defense of wild places.

COMING HOME

We uncover the canoe and the fishing gear and head back out across Cranberry Lake. It's a perfect Indian summer day, austere blue sky, astringent breeze from the north. We're paddling alongside a long, rock-rimmed wooded island when we spot a group of mallards down at the tip, a hundred yards off. Quickly, like an Iroquois hunter arranging a game drive, Dan makes a plan.

"I'll drop you on the island and paddle toward the flock," he says. "In the meantime you sneak across the island and set up an ambush. Stay hidden and stay quiet. I'm pretty sure I can get them to fly right past your hiding place."

I get off on the island, and Dan paddles slowly away. The birds move back around the tip out and of sight. Quietly, deliberately, he paddles around after them.

Stalking silently through the woods, avoiding stepping on dry twigs and leaves, I cut through the timber until I come to the narrow channel separating the island and the mainland. Crouching behind a small blown-down spruce tree where I have a good view, I settle down and wait. Perfect.

Suddenly, I hear the quack-quack and kwek-kwek of startled mallards flying up the channel right toward me. And then there they are, a good dozen of them, not twenty yards away, flying right past me. It's a perfect setup, a can't-miss proposition, but somehow I do. The ducks fly by unscathed. A single feather wafts on the breeze and settles on the dark channel, where it accuses me of complete incompetence. Dumbfounded, searching for answers, I stare at the Browning the way an outfielder who just dropped an easy pop fly stares at his mitt.

During the night the temperature sinks like a stone and an early storm drops a couple of inches of snow. In the morning, well before first light, the air is a frosty twelve degrees. Black ice is rapidly forming in the cove in front of camp. We slide the canoe across the ice to open water, then paddle in silence through the inky dark, headed for a shallow bay across the lake where we spotted ducks feeding yesterday.

We set out the decoys, arranging them with frozen hands in the numbing black water, and then we paddle to shore and drag the canoe far back into the trees. After we drape some camouflage netting over a crisscross of large fallen branches, we hunker down in the snow on our sleeping pads, pour steaming cups of coffee from the thermos, and wait for the dawn.

In the crepuscular light I watch the lake and sky with half my mind, letting the other half wander back over the country we've seen the last few days. The Cranberry Lake–Beaver River country is a pretty big place—about half a million acres—bigger than the Koyukuk Wilderness in Alaska, bigger than the Bridger Wilderness out in Wyoming, twice the size of Idaho's Sawtooth Wilderness. And it's right here, up in the rafters of the country's second-most populous state.

I never even see the birds come in. Dan's gun crashes twice and two mallards plop among the decoys. He slips out in the canoe to retrieve them, and I can see I've been away from the chase too long. My senses are dulled, I'm not as alert as I need to be. I remind myself this is serious business, that I need to pay attention. The only cure is to spend more time out here, in places like this, a perfect wilderness.

The sun strikes the nameless frosty ridge across the smoky water, lighting it with an ethereal rosy glow as snow crystals and autumn leaves mix, tumble, and scurry along the shore, hurried by the icy north wind. And this time I see them, flying low far out over the water. And then they turn, veering straight for the decoys.

PARADISE BELOW ZERO

CHESUNCOOK, MAINE

In The Maine Woods, *Henry David Thoreau wrote, "For my dessert, I helped myself to a large slice of the Chesuncook woods, and took a hearty draught of its waters with all my senses." A summer traveler, he was curious about the North Country winter, and so he jotted down what the lumbermen told him about it in his notebook: "They said that in winter the snow was three feet deep on a level here, and sometimes four or five,—that the ice on the lake was two feet thick, clear, and four feet including the snow-ice."*

As the indigo night slowly gives way to the pale rose wash of dawn, I'm standing amid a fringe of ragged black spruce mantled with fresh snow. Out on Chesuncook Lake a slashing north wind sweeps last night's snowfall into serpentine trails of powder hissing above the surface.

And then something extraordinary happens: the crimson sun bursts above the horizon, igniting the mile-high buttresses of Mount Katahdin with a startling flare, and then splits in two.

Astonished, I turn to see if anyone else is there to share the miraculous sight, but no; when it's twenty-three degrees below zero, most people aren't foolish enough to hang around outside, waiting for the sunrise.

Actually most people wouldn't be here, deep in the Maine woods in the dead of winter, at all. But then most people never see an arctic refraction shear

Alexandra Conover pulls her toboggan as a brewing January snowstorm threatens strong winds and heavy snows.

the sun into twin fireballs. They never watch, awestruck, as the ghostly banners of the aurora borealis unfurl across an icy firmament. They never see brilliant snow crystals dazzling in the sunshine like a field of diamonds.

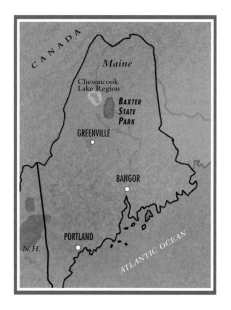

"Traveling like this is perpetual romance for me," wrote Elliott Merrick of snowshoeing with Labrador trappers during the winter of 1930. Merrick's classic narrative of that experience, *True North,* is filled with humorous, lyrical descriptions of journeying through the trackless wilderness at fifty below zero. For Merrick, that winter provided the adventures of a lifetime.

Another early-twentieth-century Labrador traveler, William Brooks Cabot, was enraptured by the winter wilds. "So it is that those of us, white and Indian, who have seen much of the interior, have always turned toward the winter trips," he wrote. "If one goes mainly for the trip itself, for the being out, there is nothing quite like the northern winter. There is the region of the elemental, there the keen air and the flash of the low sun on snow; there the rhythmic crunch of snowshoes under the northern lights and the high winter moon, the long trail that knows no willing end—*i-shipits-nan*, the Indians call it—their immemorial winter road."

But talk to many people who have spent a winter night outdoors, even under the guidance of an outdoor leadership school, and they aren't likely to describe the experience as "perpetual romance." More likely you'll hear about the "challenge" of "surviving" the "brutal conditions." Understandably, these brief, unpleasant excursions into the cold and dark usually aren't repeated.

This is unfortunate, for the often-crowded wildlands of summer revert to expansive wilderness in winter. If only there were a way to explore those crystalline landscapes without employing the high-tech siege tactics of Himalayan climbers—methods completely out of place in the Northern Forest.

Well, there is another way, and its practitioners call it "snow walking." Snow walking is a winter travel technique that evolved over centuries among the native peoples of the North. And that's why I'm here along with six others: to learn classic winter trail skills from Garrett and Alexandra Conover, Maine guides and heirs to this rich wilderness tradition. Personally, I'm especially pleased with the deep cold and snow we've encountered these past few days because I want to put their methods to a rigorous test. I figure if I can use the skills they teach me here, in the North Woods of Maine where the temperature can ratchet down to forty below zero or lower, then I can use them anywhere.

Garrett and Alexandra are exceptionally qualified to teach outdoor living skills for one very good reason: for the Conovers, the wilderness is quite literally their home—their year-round residence is a canvas wall tent pitched on a bluff above a salmon stream in northern Maine. Because they live in the woods, they are as comfortable there as the rest of us are in our living rooms.

The Conovers founded their guide service, North Woods Ways, in 1980 after apprenticing for several years with Francis "Mick" Fahey, one of the last of the old-time Maine guides. Before he died, Fahey passed on to them the arcane knowledge and woods lore he had acquired from the Penobscot Indians as a young man.

In spring, summer, and fall Garrett and Alexandra guide canoe expeditions down Maine's Allagash, Penobscot, and Saint John Rivers using elegant traditional wood-and-canvas canoes, ash setting poles, and other time-honored North Woods equipment and techniques. Poling up and down rapids, portaging pack baskets with leather tumplines, and paddling heavily laden canoes with the

The Conovers' loads slide effortlessly behind them in handmade Cree toboggans.

highly efficient and all but forgotten North Woods stroke are just some of the skills they teach between break-up and freeze-up.

With the onset of winter the Conovers switch to snowshoes and Indian toboggans, traveling the same now-frozen waterways, taking advantage of the flat, smooth surfaces that make perfect winter roads. Late winter usually finds Garrett and Alexandra traveling with Cree and Naskapi friends deep in the un-inhabited interior of northern Quebec and Labrador. Today, Garrett and Alexandra are widely considered the most skilled nonindigenous practitioners of the fine art of snow walking.

At first their winter trips were motivated by more than the mere desire to be outdoors. "We were so poor, we couldn't afford firewood," says Alexandra. "So we went where the firewood was!" For two winters in a row in the early 1980s, the Conovers set out upon two-hundred-mile-long snowshoe journeys through the Maine woods—down the frozen Saint John River and up the Al-lagash. Not only did living on the winter trail for months keep their expenses down, it gave them the chance to perfect their techniques.

Today when Garrett and Alexandra set out on a winter expedition, they decline to use state-of-the-art winter camping equipment. The gear available in specialty stores and outfitting shops is designed primarily for use in alpine areas, and it can be very awkward and inefficient when used in the North Woods environment.

So instead of sinking deep in the snow under the burden of enormous mountaineering backpacks, the Conover's loads slide effortlessly along behind them in handmade wooden Cree toboggans. Instead of slogging through deep drifts on little aluminum mountaineering snowshoes, they stride along the surface supported by traditional wide wood-and-gut Maine snowshoes. Instead of spending long, cold, boring nights in tiny nylon shelters (Garrett calls backpacking tents "sensory-deprivation chambers"), they lounge in the seventy to eighty degree warmth of spacious, woodstove-heated canvas-wall tents. Instead of forcing down a prepackaged dehydrated meal that tastes like sawdust, they feast on warm fresh-baked bread and hearty caribou stew.

After sunrise I go back inside the tent, strip off my down parka, and lean back against my stuffed sleeping bag. I shut my eyes for a moment and listen to the spruce snapping in the stove. The wood was split with a very sharp Hudson Bay cruising ax—a tool that would be considered quite inappropriate in a fragile high-altitude setting or in a tiny overused wilderness preserve. But here in the big, cold, heavily wooded wilds of Maine, or in northern Canada or Alaska, tools such as axes and firearms are essential. On one 350-mile winter traverse of Labrador, one of the most remote wilderness regions left on the planet, Garrett and Alexandra depended for their survival upon the eighty-four ptarmigan they took with their twelve-gauge shotguns and cooked over the woodstove.

Alpinists, weekend backpackers, and other casual users of what Garrett calls "postage-stamp-size wild areas" often express dismay when they hear about the Conover's methods. But rather than deflect the criticism, Garrett welcomes the chance to exchange ideas and philosophies. As we wait for the coffee to perk, I prod him with questions. Why the ax, I needle. Why the fire? Why not ditch the nineteenth-century methods and join the rest of us in the Leave-No-Trace twenty-first century?

"It's really pretty simple," says Garrett. "I believe that people who adopt high-tech gear usually subordinate themselves to it. They become dependent on the equipment and never learn to do for themselves. Folks who use complex, high-tech gear imported from the outside insulate themselves from direct engagement with their surroundings. We live in a culture which favors a

OVERLEAF:
Winter travel as perpetual romance: the Conovers crossing Maine's Umbazooksus Lake in full-blown arctic conditions.

'look-but-don't-touch' approach to nature, which requires we be aliens in wild places. Our culture says 'take only pictures, leave only footprints.' Unfortunately, for all its good intentions, that philosophy just reinforces the notion that mankind is separate from nature.

"But it doesn't have to be like that," he continues. "Look at the Naskapi and the Cree. Those are people whose woodcraft is highly developed, and they have a far deeper and much more personal understanding of the wilderness."

Voices in the Forest

I believe a person's character grows from the landscape—the plot of a novel will grow out of it as well. The smells, sounds, prevailing winds, and seasons predicate that life will be lived a certain way. The character of the people of the Northern Forest grew from such a natural landscape. Back then people cooperated with nature; they didn't try to dominate it. They recognized that their lives were connected to the land. 🌿

E. ANNIE PROULX, *Pulitzer Prize and National Book Award winning author of* The Shipping News.

And it's not as if modern gear is a panacea for the environment, he points out. "Look at lightweight backpacking stoves. Most people say, 'Don't build a fire, use a stove!' But what a 'low-impact' stove really does is displace the environmental impact. A stove user enlists a world-wide army of extractors, refiners, smelters, manufacturers, and distributors, all dealing with nonrenewable resources and contributing to toxic waste through manufacturing and transportation processes. Sure, I agree stoves have their place, and in order to conserve the small overused preserves, it's necessary to use a stove to reduce your immediate impact. But don't be fooled into thinking they are a low-impact piece of equipment!"

After a breakfast of hot black coffee, hot cereal, bacon, and bannock bread—all cooked on the woodstove—we break down the tents and load the long, narrow Cree toboggans. Made of very thin ash or maple planks held together by crossbars, the sleds are ten-to-twelve-feet long and tapered evenly from a width of about twelve inches at the front to about ten inches at the tail. Alexandra says the tapered shape helps the sleds to track swiftly behind the person pulling. We put on our snowshoes, and then lean into the pulling traces. Though loaded with upwards of seventy pounds apiece—a crushing load for a backpacker—the toboggans snake along quickly and easily, gliding in the track behind each snow walker.

Striding along the surface of the snow on my wide Maine snowshoes, pulling my toboggan, I almost feel ashamed at how little effort traveling like this requires. I can look around at the winter landscape, keep an eye out for wildlife, let my thoughts wander. Like many others, I'm so used to the "no pain, no gain" mentality that I feel as if I'm cheating. I mention this to Alexandra, who smiles and remarks that "winter backpacking may be Spartan and rigorous. But the goal here isn't to suffer. The goal here is to enjoy yourself."

We form a bright and colorful line as we pass thickly timbered Gero Island and head across Chesuncook Lake toward the West Branch of the Penobscot River. As we pass the entrance to Caucomgomac Stream, I steal a look at my teachers. Neither Conover looks the part of the stereotypical arctic explorer. Missing is the look of grim determination that characterized a Robert Peary; or the painful detachment one sees in the sad eyes of a Roald Amundsen. Instead, here are two people perfectly content in their surroundings; people for whom the popular notion of "conquering the elements" is probably both strange and disturbing.

Our home in the wilderness is a spacious, woodstove-heated canvas-wall tent. Inside, the flasks have come out, the storytelling has begun, and dinner is simmering on the stove.

The wind picks up again, driving the snow snakes that swirl around our mukluks—light Native American footwear with breathable elk-hide lowers and canvas uppers that reach like gaiters to just below the knees.

The mukluk is actually the outer shell of a layered footwear system that includes a synthetic-on-silk liner sock next to the skin, a couple of thick wool socks over the liner sock, and a thick felt boot liner—such as is used in snowmobile boots or rubber Pac boots—over the wool socks. Designed for snowshoeing in extremely cold temperatures, mukluks keep feet warm, dry, and comfortable. The contrast with stiff modern boots weighing three or four times as much is startling. As that veteran Labrador traveler, William Brooks Cabot, observed, "The tale of the winter trail is the tale of one's feet." Dry feet are warm feet, and warm feet are happy feet. Right now my feet are happy, and so am I. Why, I wonder, do the boot makers keep producing heavy winter boots made of plastic or rubber—materials that trap cold, clammy moisture right next to the foot? Don't they know people like to be comfortable?

I realize that I'm beginning to think like a snow walker.

As the pallid winter sun sinks gently into the cradling tops of the stunted black spruce, we set up camp on the edge of the trees. Soon the stoves are snapping and smoke is rising from the stovepipes and wafting into the frigid night air. The lake ice booms as it contracts and shifts. Trees crack and pop like fireworks in the cold.

Inside, as we prepare dinner, we talk about the mysterious fate of the Franklin Expedition to the Northwest Passage. We talk about the "Golden Age" of polar exploration, about Amundsen, Scott, and Peary. Eventually, we talk about what is happening right here in the Northern Forest. Even though he is by nature an optimist, always ready with a quip and a grin, Garrett is doubtful about the future of the Great North Woods.

"For me," he says, "it all comes down to numbers. We humans are like the deer on Mount Desert Island feasting on the unnaturally lush growth that sprouted after the 1947 fire. Now the growth is gone and the deer are starving to death. The population problem is so frightening. We are like the goat herders at the edge of the Sahara, spreading desertification thirty miles per year, every year. It's the tragedy of the commons. There is virtually no plausible solution."

I reach over and add a few honey-colored strips of split spruce to the stove. After all my travels through the region, I'm surprised to hear someone speak with such honest skepticism about the future of the Great North Woods, to hear someone who doesn't feel a need to parrot the pro forma assertions that

everything will work out just fine in the end.

"The paper companies who own the land aren't looking much past the next few years," Garrett continues. "When they pull out, and they will pull out, will it be a free-for-all or a responsible reckoning?"

One of the other clients on the trip, Randy, a man in his thirties from Tennessee on his first winter expedition, asks Garrett what people can do. Garrett replies, "I think you have to work where you feel you can be effective. But you can't waste energy worrying. Right now I think the only solution is to go live in a wall tent at the north end of Chesuncook Lake. You have to be fatalistic. Until we understand that our population just can't keep expanding exponentially, there is virtually nothing that can be done."

Outside in the brittle cold a chorus of coyotes yips at the bone-white sliver of moon.

Relaxing by the fire in a traditional tent-fire camp.

And then a longer, deeper, melancholy howl issues from the forest. Stunned, I slip out of the tent into the frosty night. The mournful cry stops me in midstride. There aren't supposed to be any wolves in Maine. *Are there?* Again the deep, sonorous notes issue from the heavy timber a hundred yards or so behind the tent. I stand stock-still, holding my breath for long moments, but the sound fades in the crisp night air.

After several more minutes of intense listening, I turn back toward the tent. It's a cheery point of light in the vast black wilderness, glowing from within by the light of candles, the sound of laughter, and the warmth of friendship. Inside, the flasks have come out, the storytelling has resumed, and dinner is simmering on the stove.

KATAHDIN

The Weather in Baxter State Park can be severe and it can change drastically. . . . Trails may become impassable due to heavy snow. . . . Wind above treeline can make travel impossible. The wind can also move large amounts of snow quickly, loading it onto leeward slopes to create dangerous avalanche conditions. . . . All climbers should be prepared for an emergency bivouac if necessary.

—BAXTER STATE PARK AUTHORITY, MAINE

On a sparkling February day I pull a sled heavily laden with camping gear and provisions up a steep, snowy trail in Maine's Baxter State Park. The path winds before me, writhing like a white serpent through the evergreen forest. The landscape is still—nothing moves, except for me—and silence engulfs me. The only sounds I hear are the swishing of my skis, the tap of my poles, and my own heavy breathing. Even the other members of my group are somewhere behind me and out of sight. No doubt they are enjoying the sense of wilderness solitude as much as I am.

More rocky than the Rockies, Katahdin's infamous Knife Edge rises above a group of winter mountaineers on a crisp February day.

Here and there, the immaculate surface of the trail is marred by the great plunging tracks of moose. I pause, trying to decipher the text of their erratic wanderings. After a few moments I again lean into my harness, feeling my sled slide along the slick surface behind me. Then I raise my eyes from the trail ahead and see the jagged ramparts of Katahdin through gaps in the stolid conifers. The massive peak thrusts upward into a flawless arch of blue sky.

The sight thrills me to the core, inspires me to take one more stride, and then another. Soon I am lost in thought, reflecting upon an earlier traveler's journey to Katahdin, a word meaning "greatest mountain" in the Penobscot Indian language.

Henry David Thoreau attempted to climb Katahdin in 1846. Just shy of the summit the clouds closed around him, blotting out the sky, and cold winds swept the stark moonscape of the pinnacle ridge. Pamola, the howling storm god of the Penobscot was there, beating his wings, kicking up a tempest. Half man, half eagle, Pamola still wields the power to destroy those who venture into his blustery domain. Writing of his experience in *The Maine Woods,* Thoreau recalled that "Pamola is always angry with those who climb to the summit of Ktaadn."

Little has changed in the intervening century and a half. Katahdin still stands indomitable above the wilderness of northern Maine. At any time of year the mountain may humble even the best equipped climbing parties. But in winter, when temperatures plunge into the minus forties and winter storms drop heavy loads of snow, the mountain is an especially stern reminder of human frailty.

At 5,267 feet, Katahdin is the centerpiece of Baxter State Park, a 314-square-mile chunk of protected wilderness in the heart of Maine's fabled North Woods.

Katahdin is a peak of steep slopes and rugged glacial cirques, of vast alpine tablelands and sharply serrated ridges, some stretching more than four miles from the summit. Remote and austere, Katahdin's massive front rises sharply 4,500 feet above the surrounding boreal forest, rivers, and lakes of the park; and it watches over a constellation of lesser peaks, eighteen of which rise above 3,500 feet. Merely to reach the base of the great mountain in winter is a two-day, fourteen-mile ski through the surrounding forest.

On Katahdin, Thoreau encountered a surreal wasteland, a Nature far different than the gentle one he knew from wandering the forests and fields of Concord. Instead, on Katahdin he found "a barren, forbidding place, vast, savage, and awful . . . ultimately unknowable . . . the raw, unyielding face of Nature, indifferent to humans." Here, for the first time, he encountered a free, untamed land, a place with a wild spirit not yet made subservient to human cupidity. On Katahdin, he realized, Nature was physically awesome yet deadly and uncaring. He wrote that the mountain seemed to confront him, demanding: "Why came ye here before your time? Why seek me when I have not called thee? Should thou freeze or starve or shudder thy life away, here is no shrine, no altar, nor any access to my ear."

Terrified, yet strangely elated from this brush with a power greater than any he had known, Thoreau retreated from Katahdin. The encounter caused him to examine the very nature of his own existence: "Talk of mysteries!" he wrote. "Think of our life in nature, daily to be shown matter, to come in contact with it—rocks, trees, wind on our cheeks! The solid earth! The actual world. The common sense. Contact! Contact! Who are we? Where are we?"

As evening descends, the temperature drops with the pale sun. The surface of the snow, which had softened during the short daylight hours, begins to harden. The trail continues to rise, entering a stand of northern hardwoods.

Birch, beech, maple, and ash emerge from the snow that lies like a soft cloak upon the land. Chickadees flit among the branches, seemingly oblivious to the cold. Cool blue shadows flung down by the tall trees stretch across the snow like giant fingers, pointing the way to Roaring Brook and camp for the night.

At Roaring Brook the lean-to shelters used by throngs of carefree warm-weather campers lie hushed beneath five-foot mounds of snow. The brook, whose numerous swim holes host the happy splashing of children during the summer season, now lies still, locked tight in ice. There is a peaceful tranquillity to the scene that most visitors never experience. I quickly unpack my sled, put on a heavy down parka, and begin the process of melting snow water for dinner on a camp stove. While the water warms to a boil my partners ski into camp, singly and in pairs, until all ten of us are reunited once again. Soon we gather around the little flame, drawn together by the warm food, the hot drinks, and the desire for companionship in the midst of the vast, brooding silence.

Voices in the Forest

This land has a rich cultural heritage—the Native Americans, Thoreau, the old sporting camps, those things should be factored in, taken into account. You can't replicate wilderness with a theme park or a boardwalk. People must understand they are a part of nature. Without wilderness, how will they ever understand that?

JERRY STELMOK, *builder of hand-made canoes and author of* Building the Maine Guide Canoe *and* The Wood & Canvas Canoe.

We are here to explore Baxter State Park in winter, the dominant season in northern Maine. Most years the snow starts to fly in November and doesn't stop until April. The ice usually doesn't go out of the big lakes until May. Consequently, the bulk of the park's visitors arrive during the short summer season. During the long winter the park sleeps, visited by only a handful of intrepid adventurers with the skills to negotiate the rugged terrain and the inhospitable climate. To keep the unwary and the unskilled from falling victim to Pamola, the Baxter State Park Authority strictly limits access to the park in winter, and all prospective winter visitors must apply for a permit from park headquarters.

From the Basin Ponds, the trail climbs sharply to Chimney Pond, where we plan to make a base camp for the next five or six days. As I climb, I fix my eyes on the skis of the person ahead, watching them slowly ascend the slippery slope. Mesmerized by the repetitive step-and-slide, step-and-slide motion, the miles pass. The skis ahead somehow appear to pull me up the slope. I call this bewitching phenomenon "visual draft." There may be no scientific basis for my belief in the success of this effect, but it has hauled me up many a mountain over the years.

Finally, after hours of struggle in the steep, soft snow, we top a rise and emerge from the forest. Ice-covered Chimney Pond lies before us like a gemstone in a tooled granite setting. We set up camp at the base of a gigantic amphitheater, an enormous horseshoe-shaped cirque chiseled out of the mountains by glaciers during the last ice age fifteen thousand years ago. On all sides precipitous walls soar to sharply serrated ridgelines; and from the ridges ice-falls and snow gullies swoop at radical angles back down to the basin floor. The scene is impossibly alpine, more rocky than the Rockies.

That night, under a wondrous display of northern lights dancing above the mountain rim, I curl up in my sleeping bag with a hot drink and read the history of the mountain and the park by the light of my headlamp. I agree with the description of an early climber, William Larrabee, who in the nineteenth century portrayed Katahdin as "rising from a vast forest plain, like an island from an illimitable ocean."

Lying far beyond the coastal villages, Katahdin remained hidden behind the unbroken north woods for more than a century and a half after the European settlement of Maine's shores.

The first description of Katahdin was given by an explorer named Joseph Chadwick, who metaphorically pulled away the evergreen shield hiding the peak in 1763. After his fleeting glimpse, however, the forest closed in again, once more presenting a formidable barrier to exploration and cloaking Katahdin in mystery for another forty years. The great mountain was forgotten, lapsing into myth and legend until rediscovery by the first official exploration of Maine's interior in 1804, the same year Lewis and Clark were dispatched to investigate the country's new lands far to the west.

Katahdin's highest point is called Baxter Peak, after the former governor of Maine, Percival Baxter. Baxter was an original thinker, a man who called himself a political conservative but a social progressive. As a turn-of-the-century college student he was an original hippie, had been jailed at political

---

Voices in the Forest

I feel that many physical things about the landscape here agree with me: the long low sea of hills, the fuzzy anonymous forest, the relative isolation of these mountains. And there are metaphorical aspects about this place—it's a second chance wilderness. There's something special about a place that is saved through human choice.

BILL MCKIBBEN, *former staff writer for the* New Yorker *and author of* The End of Nature *and* Maybe One.

OPPOSITE:

The mountains of the Northern Forest have provided challenge and excitement to many of the country's best alpinists for generations.

rallies, and been called a "long-hair" in the press. Nevertheless, he matured into a formidable political force, and became one of Maine's most popular governors. He worked tirelessly throughout his life to ensure that Katahdin and the surrounding lands would be protected from the insatiable logging practices that he felt threatened to destroy them.

From the mid-1800s on, much of the Maine woods was heavily and repeatedly cut over. In 1895 a coalition of civic leaders, business groups, and newspaper editors actually called for the creation of a state park to save the woods and mountains from further desecration. The legislature refused, and the deforestation continued essentially unabated. Outraged, Baxter took the matter into his own hands.

Over the course of thirty years Baxter bought the mountain and encircling forestlands from the timber companies who owned, and still own, most of the northern portion of the state. During the first three decades of the 1900s he bought more than three hundred square miles of land that he then transferred to the people of Maine under the proviso that "they shall be forever left in the wild natural state."

"The works of men are short-lived," said Baxter. "Monuments decay, buildings crumble, wealth vanishes, but Katahdin and its massive grandeur will forever remain the mountain of the people of Maine." In 1933 the state legislature, which had refused to contribute a cent to the purchase, named the park in Baxter's honor.

Morning dawns clear, calm, and frigid—around twenty-five degrees below zero. Despite the cold, Pamola appears to be resting, and it is a perfect day to sneak a summit attempt. We quickly don boots and crampons; grab ice axes and climbing ropes; pack food, water, and extra clothes; and set out for the Cathedral Trail winding up toward the skyline.

Partway up the Cathedral Trail we pass the scene of an avalanche that swept a climber to his death several years ago. We stop and contemplate the scene, looking at the rock rubble and snapped tree limbs left by the slide. Then we look across the cirque to the Pamola Ice Cliffs spilling down the opposite side of the rocky amphitheater. One January day in 1974 a party of six experienced climbers were caught on a ledge by a horrific storm. They were unable to move up or down as snow pelted the mountain and the temperature dropped to thirty below zero. One of the climbers died, another suffered major frostbite and subsequently the loss of a limb.

We shift our view above the Pamola Ice Cliffs, to the infamous Knife Edge. There, a Baxter State Park ranger disappeared during an October blizzard in 1964. Despite a massive search, his body was never found. These and other events are a part of the park's lore, and most every winter climber knows the stories.

On the final approach to the summit cairn, the snow is a blinding white as we crunch across it, feeling the secure bite of our crampons with each step. It is indeed a rare day, clear, blue, cold, without a trace of cloud. From our lofty perch we can look out over Baxter State Park and millions of acres of Maine woods. Turning to absorb the 360-degree view, I recall Thoreau's words from the flanks of this same mountain a century and a half ago: "From this elevation," he wrote, "just on the skirts of the clouds, we could overlook the country . . . for a hundred miles. There it was, the State of Maine. . . . Immeasurable forest. . . . Countless lakes . . . like a mirror broken into a thousand fragments, and wildly scattered . . . reflecting the full blaze of the sun."

The view of the park from high atop Katahdin is essentially unchanged since Thoreau's day. The scars left by the early lumbermen have had time to heal. I join the others in a slow procession across the icy, precipitous Knife Edge, looking down a thousand feet on either side. Despite Thoreau's assurances that on Katahdin, "certainly men would live forever, and laugh at death and the grave," I am quite confident that a slip here would be mighty costly. And so I concentrate on the placement of each step, occasionally stopping to look out upon the vast panorama of frozen lakes and sugary forests far below, and down upon the sharp blade of ice, rock, and snow beneath my boots.

Hours later, back down at Chimney Pond, I look up at Baxter Peak and think about the vision and philanthropy of Percival P. Baxter. And I wonder if his like will ever be seen again in the Northern Forest.

THE ONE HUNDRED MILE
WILDERNESS

"Saw 2 shooting stars and a beaver, and the coyotes howled in the distance. This morn-
ing I got my fill of lush red ripe raspberries, saw the 2 moose, the bullfrogs, and the loon-
like bird. Another day in the magical forest. Ahh Maine! This is a beautiful place with
great vibes and I wish everyone who passes this way experiences beyond description."

APPALACHIAN TRAIL HIKER,

FROM THE REGISTER AT RAINBOW STREAM LEAN-TO

THE SOUND OF A VOICE drifts over me from somewhere beyond the pe-
riphery of my awareness.

"...in the pond!"

I mumble something in response, then roll over into the warm, soft downy
folds of my sleeping bag. But the voice will not be ignored. It pursues me,
piercing my murky subconscious in an unsettling way, like a searchlight prob-
ing a still, dark night.

"In the pond. A MOOSE!"

Slowly I rise from the depths to break the plane of awareness. My eyes pop
open and register the soft light of a late-summer Maine morning along the Appalachian Trail. A bearded face is peering down at me from above. The face is
sputtering something about a moose in the pond. The eyes above the beard are
wild, excited, fanatic.

"MOOSE!" Shouts the face.

The
Appalachian
Trail crosses a
stream in the
heart of the
One Hundred
Mile
Wilderness.

"Of course there's a moose in the pond, you dolt!" I think, yawning. "This is Maine!"

I shut my eyes and try to sleep again, thinking this guy would excitedly tell a farmer there's a cow in his pasture, but it's too late. The spell is broken, my brain has been booted-up. The inevitable data flood begins to wash across my mental screen, beginning with the identity of the face above me. It reads:

Name: Ringo

Age: Twentyish

Occupation: Appalachian Trail thru-hiker

Location: 100 Mile Wilderness, Maine

Last Seen: Previous evening, camped in an abandoned fire tower atop Barren Mountain.

I surrender. "Good morning, Ringo. Sleep well?"

A quick check tells me that my tent mate and partner on this adventure, photographer Peter Cole, is not yet with us. A swift elbow jab fixes that.

"Good morning, Peter. There's a moose in the pond."

"Of course there's a moose in the pond," he replies sleepily, eyes still clamped firmly shut. "This is Maine." Peter checks out again. I sense he is not sufficiently impressed. I give Ringo a "what can you do?" look. He shrugs.

"Of course there's a moose in the pond," says Peter. "This is Maine."

I have no choice but to get up, since Ringo seems to have appointed me official inspector of moose ponds along this portion of the Appalachian Trail.

"Thanks Ringo," I say, pulling on my boots. "Now where's that moose?"

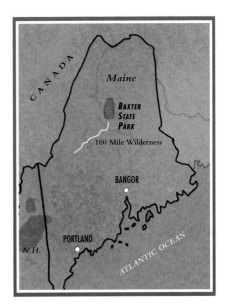

Had a moose walk right through camp towards the stream.

—ONE HUNDRED MILE WILDERNESS HIKER, FROM THE TRAIL REGISTER AT WADLEIGH STREAM LEAN-TO

Ringo's moose is knee deep in Cloud Pond, a well-named glacial tarn, one of three clear, cold mountain lakes sitting high atop the vapor rending spine of the range. This bull moose, his palmate headgear gleaming in the soft morning light, is enjoying a leisurely breakfast of luscious aquatic weeds. A young fellow, judging from his moderate size, he acknowledges our presence with an occasional impassive glance but otherwise pays us no attention.

Moose make good use of this section of the Appalachian Trail in New England. There's plenty of water, timber, and cool breeze to keep biting flies at bay. Tracks and spoor are frequently encountered on the footpath. You never know where you're going to bump into one.

The moose's head goes down with a splash as he tears juicy succulents from the lake bottom. Then, when he raises his head, water cascades from his rack down his neck and back with the sound of a small waterfall. There are tender green shoots hanging out both sides of his mouth. Ringo, Peter, and I have breakfast together pond-side and watch the moose until he wanders off on other business, whereupon we shoulder our packs and hit the trail.

This northernmost section of the Appalachian Trail is truly in the Big Woods, a region of some fifteen million acres officially known as the "Unorganized Territories" of Maine. For a hundred miles the trail snakes through the woods, climbs the mountains, and skirts the "ponds." In Maine, if you can see the opposite shore, it's called a pond. But not once in that entire distance does the trail cross a paved road. The One Hundred Mile Wilderness is the longest stretch of the entire 2,100 mile Appalachian Trail with no paved road crossings.

Were the region set aside as a national forest, it would dwarf all others in the contiguous United States. You could stash five or six Yellowstones here and still have room for a Yosemite or two. But unlike national parks, there are no visitor centers, no scenic loops, no "attractions." This is wild country on an Alaskan or Canadian scale, right in the heart of Maine.

The One Hundred Mile Wilderness begins outside the tiny village of Monson in the center of the state. The trail then winds north across a quilt of managed forests, conservation holdings, and state and federal lands. At the West Branch of the Penobscot River the trail crosses a paved logging road, officially the end of the One Hundred Mile Wilderness section, then plunges back into the forest and begins the fourteen-mile climb to the summit of Katahdin, the famed glacial-scoured monolith that marks the northern terminus of the Appalachian Trail.

OPPOSITE:
A waterfall
tumbles along
side the trail
deep in the One
Hundred Mile
Wilderness.

But it's moose that occupy our thoughts this morning, not Katahdin. After our encounter with the moose at Cloud Pond, Peter and I break camp and amble north beneath a sea of gray, scuddy clouds. Despite the incandescent sunset of the night before and the implied promise of fair weather today, we are rapidly becoming socked-in. Unfortunately, this looks like of one of those low pressure systems that settles over Maine and hangs for a week or two dropping rain or snow until it leisurely counter-rotates itself into oblivion over Labrador or out to sea.

The temperature is in the mid-fifties, tops, a fairly typical late-summer day—raw and wet. In fact, this region is one of the coldest and wettest in all of North America, as evidenced by the vegetation. The trail is lined with caribou moss, which looks like a white mat of twined antlers. And there's winterberry, bunchberry, and the pale wispy strands of old man's beard draped in the sweet smelling balsams. These remind me that in a few months the temperature may be 100 degrees colder than it is today. Even on this trip a white flake or two will remind us that winter is never far off.

The lichen-covered rocks where the trail crosses exposed ridges are slick, and we both take a slide now and then. In the ravines, where we tread on a soft, silent layer of needles and humus, the spruce and fir forest is dark and quiet, its spirit present but elusive.

These are among the oldest mountains in the world. They are part of

the chain formed some 450 million years ago, when the drifting continents of Europe and North America collided. The concussion from that encounter, and another that occurred about 300 million years ago when Africa slammed into North America, created the Appalachians, a mountain range some 1,500 miles long stretching from Quebec's Gaspe Peninsula to the highlands of central Alabama.

Over the years natural forces have given the mountains their present aspect. Here in northern New England the Appalachians were overridden more than once by glaciers up to two miles thick. These glaciers cut and gouged the range, creating the characteristic cirques, U-shaped valleys, and scoured bedrock ridges, as well as the countless lakes, ponds, and wetlands.

Make no mistake. These mountains aren't as high as they once were, for in their youth they rivaled the Himalayas, but they are a rough, rowdy bunch. They'll lure you up with a series of false summits, rip the clouds and wow you with a flamboyant view, then slam-dunk you down a knee-pounding rockfall, deep into a fathomless col, only to bottom out in wet sphagnum and start you right back up again. Unlike kinder, gentler ranges, these mountains are relentless. They never level off for long, even on the ridgelines. Hiking here is like tramping the scalloped edge of a stone blade. The elevation gain on the One Hundred Mile Wilderness northbound is a surprising, heart-thumping, 17,000 feet. And yet mountains make up perhaps only half the total distance.

> I saw a pine marten for the first time yesterday. It looked like a dark brown, bushy tailed ferret with big round ears.
> —ONE HUNDRED MILE WILDERNESS HIKER,
> FROM THE RAINBOW STREAM LEAN-TO

Unlike footpaths in other parts of the country, this trail we're on is of relatively recent vintage—middle aged, really. Two fellows named Myron Avery

---

Voices in the Forest

There are plenty of people up here that have no idea there's an Appalachian Trail. They would no more put on a pair of hiking boots than you and I would drive through Manhattan. People see out-of-state plates parked at trailheads and they feel they aren't welcome in their own forest. For the folks up here, the woods have always been a place to make a living and shoot game. 🌲

JOHN HARRIGAN, *Coos County, NH, newspaper publisher, sportsman, and columnist.*

In the One Hundred Mile Wilderness, "wind-sucking" climbs are balanced by stretches of "daydream hiking," "The kind where you don't have to watch where you put your feet."

and Walter Green cut their way through this implacable terrain in the early 1930s in an all-out push to link up with the rest of the new Appalachian Trail. Avery, a native of Lubec, Maine, was determined that the Appalachian Trail would reach Katahdin, and not end at New Hampshire's Mount Washington, as had been suggested.

Hiking along in the gloomy mist, looking at the silver beads of moisture covering everything, I think of the cairn atop Katahdin marking the end of the Appalachian Trail. That last day when he took the final trail sign out of his pack, Avery looked at his two companions, then supposedly uttered this singular dedication speech: "Nail it up." And that was that. A real Mainer, that Avery. Direct.

Another reason why hiking is a recent phenomenon here is evident from the trail. The maze of waterways viewed from the heights is a reminder that this is unsurpassed canoe country. For thousands of years the Penobscot and Passamaquoddy and their ancestors refined the art of ca-

noecraft here, by these lakeshores and streamsides. So why hike? You can get almost anywhere in Maine by canoe—upstream, downstream, through the rapids, or across the lake. You can even get out to the coastal islands for lobster. The canoe is to Maine what the horse is to Wyoming: the traditional way to travel outdoors, a symbol of local culture. Hiking, on the other hand, never had as strong an economic purpose as canoe travel, and so it remains a somewhat foreign activity, something that mostly tourists from "Away" come here to do. As one local fellow in a bar in Monson put it when he heard of our plans: "Why the heck would you want to walk all the way to Katahdin?" he asked, incredulous.

Before Avery and Green, someone—a timber cruiser surveying the woods for the lumber companies perhaps, or a solitary Penobscot on a personal quest—may have wandered among these crags and ridges, who knows? Perhaps not. In any event, no one lingered for long. Except for widely scattered outposts, these forests were never settled by Europeans or Americans. Later, the flood tide of American settlement rose to the south and then beyond this remote wild island. Men came here to cut the timber, every stick of it. But the rush to develop and settle the continent followed the setting sun.

"This section of the Appalachian Trail has the best swim holes in over 2,000 miles!" exclaimed one thru-hiker.

The next day, Peter and I follow the serpentine trail as it snakes upward toward the top of White Cap Mountain through a dwindling forest of unfurling white birch, thick sphagnum moss, and hardy wood sorrel. Above, ragged scraps of gray clouds ride the north wind, racing their dark shadows across the summit ridge. Crouching in the shelter of a subalpine fir thicket perched on the frost-shattered rock, we stop to put on our pile hats, gloves, and shell layers. Venturing above treeline is going to be a chilly and adventurous affair.

Just below the bald, cone-shaped summit we hunker down out of the wind behind a huge boulder to grab a handful of peanuts, sip a cup of hot cocoa, and soak in the view from on high. We're in a mood to linger—there is plenty of time to cover the miles to our next camp. But if we don't quite make it, if we fall short of our goal—well, we'll camp somewhere else. After all, I muse while munching a chocolate bar, the whole point of these trips is to get away from schedules and deadlines.

Reclining on my big, stuffed backpack—truly a house with shoulder straps—I discover that I am lying on a carpet of blueberries. Nibbling the juicy fruit, I contemplate our sheltering boulder. The size of a small truck, it was surely pried from the peak when the last ice age overrode this peak. I look out and envision that fabulous two-mile-thick sheet of ice cutting and scraping the land, chiseling the valleys, and generally wreaking havoc with the landscape. As Peter and I dawdle over lunch, our eyes sweep over the endless green forest reaching deep into Canada, over the myriad lakes sparkling in the brilliant sunshine like sprinkled shards of broken glass.

I fall asleep for a moment—a quick nap is a luxury to indulge in on long backpacking trips—and when I awake we have company. He introduces himself by his thru-hiker trail name, Mountain Goat. With shaggy white hair and white beard he looks every bit the high-country denizen. But this is no ordinary goat. On the far side of sixty, he has hiked more than two thousand miles—all the way to Katahdin from Springer Mountain in Georgia, the start of the Appalachian Trail.

The Goat is an unreconstructed Reb from South Carolina, and Peter and I are bluebelly Yanks from New Hampshire, but we chat easily for a half hour or so. The fact that we're from different generations and different regions matters not in the least. We're just long-distance hikers enjoying the simple camaraderie of the hills. Sharing stories and snacks, we have some good laughs, and then he shoulders his big pack.

"How far are you hiking, Goat?" I call after him.

"Back to Georgia!" he shouts over his shoulder.

The trail casts a kind of spell. After only a few days, the Maine woods starts to work its magic. One day blends seamlessly into the next as cares slip away and the outside world seems at first distant, then irrelevant, and is ultimately forgotten altogether. Hiking here becomes a way of life, the woods a home, and fellow hikers and other creatures form a close circle of friends and family.

"I love the North Woods," says Hyperman, a thru-hiker we meet while gathering blueberries in the arctic tundra on top of a long, wind-swept ridgeline. "Big forests, rushing streams, swim holes, ponds, mountain lakes with timbered shores and dotted islands, it's got it all."

Here is the mix, the potent concoction, that makes this trail experience

Voices in the Forest

There is no future in commercial forestry the way the big companies do it. When they clear-cut they are going to get less productivity, less fiber, and they will eventually find it isn't economically viable. The biggest problem with clear-cutting is that you get too much of the wrong kind of regeneration—light loving trees like popple and gray birch. The companies clear-cut, which promotes popple, but since they want softwood they have to spray herbicides to kill the popple. ❦

MEL AMES, *an advocate of stewardship and selective logging, has been cutting his 600 acres in Maine for nearly fifty years.*

OVERLEAF:
Mount Katahdin, the terminus of the Appalachian Trail, rises above the West Branch of the Penobscot River.

so splendid: it does have it all. At the West Branch of the Pleasant River, Peter and I wade across one of several wide, rushing, knee-deep flows that will pin you down and refuse passage if you catch them at high water. A solemn stand of ancient old-growth hemlock and white pine guards a chasm animated by a series of uproarious pool-drop waterfalls, "the best swim holes in over 2,000 miles of trail!" according to Rastabear, another northbound thru-hiker. Wind-sucking climbs are balanced by stretches of "daydream hiking" as Captain Moonpie calls it. "The kind where you don't have to watch where you put your feet." Elsewhere, the trail winds silently through the hush of a ghost forest—relics of giant, wind-thrown trees reposing under a thick green carpet of moss. In such places I am careful not to make a sound.

Dramatic as the mountains and whirlpools are, it is the mix of lakes and forest I find most enchanting. At Mountain Pond I watch for an hour as an enormous bull moose and a small cow moose feed together in the afterglow of evening. The soft light renders his broad, rosy antlers almost translucent. At Antlers Camp, an old logging camp falling back into the earth, I sit in the breeze under tall red pines as another storm brews. I watch and listen as mated loons call back and forth across the broad waters of Lower Jo-Mary Lake.

The soothing sound of the stream put me to sleep (or was it the hard hike?).

—ONE HUNDRED MILE WILDERNESS HIKER,
FROM THE RAINBOW STREAM LEAN-TO

There's a rare break in the clouds directly overhead, but I know better. "Sucker hole," I think as I splash across another stream and feel the frigid water wrap my lower legs like a cold compress. Sure enough, as Peter and I lope up the bank and plunge back into the forest, the clouds return, swirling across the face of the sun, unleashing a spattering of raindrops.

We step into a dank, muddy clearing. The smell of wet, raw earth and bleeding sap fills our nostrils. A fresh logging road not marked on our maps lies across our path. Giant tires have left parallel gouges deep in the soft, brown mud. Off in the distance, carried on the wind with the smell of diesel and burned oil, we hear the low-geared roar of a log skidder crashing through the understory.

OPPOSITE:
A backpacker sets up his tent at sunset after another long day of hiking on the Appalachian Trail.

We are brusquely reminded that if we step beyond the "beauty strip," the facade of trees to the left and right of the trail corridor, we may cross back into the "Industrial Forest," as the international paper companies commonly refer to northern Maine. On some of the vast forest tracts adjacent to the trail, clear-cut logging continues.

Peter and I cross the road and reenter the forest, where once again the crimson and green of hobblebush reaches out to us from beside the footpath.

This trail, this cross-section of the Maine woods, is evidence of what these forests once were. The path celebrates the Big Woods and the ancient, wise, and sustaining relationship between us and the land.

At the Wadleigh Stream shelter, listening to the rain drum on the tin roof of the lean-to, I bundle up in my sleeping bag, pour a steaming mug of hot tea,

and read the testimony of those who have passed this way. Thank goodness for the shelter! If we were out there in Peter's leaky old tent we would be in trouble. But now, who cares? Let it rain! My headlamp beam cuts the impenetrable, cavelike darkness as I scan these lines from the register:

> I'm just lovin' this Maine wilderness. The loons have taken my soul. I will never forget this time, place, or all the friends and folks I've met along the way.

Precisely. I snap off the light and fall fast asleep.

135

THE KILLER MOUNTAINS

WHERE WINTER LIVES

The average daily temperature in January hovers around 4 degrees Fahrenheit, with winds blowing at an average speed of more than 45 miles per hour (gusting to hurricane force regularly). Fog and blowing snow can reduce visibility to 200 feet or less. The wind chill equivalent frequently dips to -50 degrees Fahrenheit.

—Mount Washington Observatory

THE SUMMIT RIDGE of New Hampshire's Presidential Range is socked in. The air temperature hovers around 0 degrees, the wind blows at a steady thirty to forty miles per hour with occasional stronger gusts, and heavy snow zips horizontally through the air.

The flakes slam into me like Styrofoam pellets, bounce off, and go streaking on their way. All-in-all, it's a fairly run-of-the-mill midwinter day on Mount Washington, at 6,288 feet the highest peak in the northeastern United States and the centerpiece of the 770,000-acre White Mountain National Forest.

Darby Field of Exeter, New Hampshire, made the first recorded ascent of Mount Washington in 1642. Since then countless others have made the climb, including many world-class mountaineers who train here because the conditions on the mountain are so challenging. The peripatetic Henry David Thoreau tramped these peaks in 1839 and again in 1858. On the latter trip Thoreau took a nasty spill when he slipped on a steep patch of snow—in July.

Peter Kavouksorian snaps off of a perfect telemark turn in a very tight, very steep gully in Oaks Gulf, New Hampshire, in May.

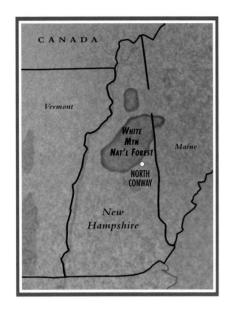

The oldest hiking trail in the United States, the Crawford Path, was blazed on Mount Washington in 1819, and today, adventuring in the Presidentials is more popular than ever. Although we seem to have the summits all to ourselves on this journey, some seven million people visit the White Mountain National Forest each year—more than converge upon Yellowstone and Yosemite National Parks combined.

A hundred years ago, few would have foreseen these mountains becoming such a popular destination. Back then, the mountainsides were blighted and barren from cut-and-run logging. And then the fuel-rich slash piles left behind by the loggers ignited, causing enormous and highly destructive fires. The era of waste and desolation ended in 1911 with the passage of the Weeks Act, legislation authorizing the federal purchase of private lands. The law ultimately led to the creation of the White Mountain National Forest and the recovery of these once bleak and depressing scenes.

Right now, typical day or not, I feel like I am standing precisely in the center of a raging tempest. Somewhere just off to my left, but hidden in the

PRECEDING
OVERLEAF:
The Presidential Range rises above the Mount Washington Valley in New Hampshire at sunrise in early December.

Winter mountaineers hike through a stand of frosted conifers at treeline in the Presidential Range.

storm, is the summit of Mount Washington. Somewhere not very far ahead of me is Joe Lentini, mountain guide and long-time director of the EMS Climbing School in North Conway, New Hampshire. And somewhere not very far behind me is the rest of our little group—Liz, Sophie, Grant, and Paul. We are attempting to complete a midwinter traverse of the mountain range that is notorious for being home to some of the world's most dangerous weather.

In these conditions every step is a well-thought-out process. I place one foot forward, setting the teeth of my crampons securely into the ice. Without them I would skitter and slide over the frost-shattered and rime-ice coated shards of the ridge. Then, planting my ski poles ahead and to the sides, I brace

A winter mountaineer hikes the moonscape of rock, ice, and snow above treeline in the Presidential Range in February.

141

against the frigid jackhammer blasts. Like the outriggers on a Tahitian canoe, the poles keep me from capsizing.

At this moment, I don't need anyone to remind me that the winter weather in the Presidential Range is simply ferocious, and that the brutal conditions here accurately mimic what only the Polar Regions and the highest mountains on earth experience. Winter temperatures up here are frequently far below zero Fahrenheit. The lowest temperature ever recorded on Mount Washington was a brisk 47 degrees below, and the mercury can dip into the minus 40 range anytime during the months of December, January, February, and March. To make matters even more challenging, these frigid temperatures are frequently accompanied by very high winds that can send the wind-chill factor plummeting and flash-freeze any exposed skin.

These fierce winter winds regularly top 100 miles per hour, once blowing at a record-setting, anemometer-smashing 231 miles per hour—the highest surface wind speed ever clocked on Earth. That gust was more than three

times the speed of a hurricane (a hurricane is a wind of 74 miles per hour or greater). Midwinter winds average between 40 and 50 miles per hour on a daily basis, and hurricane gusts are measured four or five times per week on average.

And just to top things off, there's the snow. Generally, four or five feet of snow piles up during each winter month. Nearly 570 inches of snow fell on Mount Washington during the winter of 1968-1969, still the all-time record for a single year. And by springtime it is not unusual for 70, 80, and even 100 feet of wind-deposited snow to accumulate in Tuckerman Ravine, on the east side of the range.

The heavy snow causes catastrophic avalanches not only in the steep, tree-less areas but in the lower wooded areas as well. The deep snow in the forest obscures hiking trails and blazes; while up high the blowing, drifting snow can limit visibility to a matter of a few feet in any direction and bury the rock cairns marking the trails above treeline.

The result of these violent meteorological conditions is a moonscape of rock, ice, and of course snow. Little besides tiny ground-hugging arctic tundra vegetation survives. That's no surprise, since this is the arctic, ecologically speaking. In the Presidential Range, every 400-foot elevation gain is comparable to traveling 100 miles north. We have climbed some 5,000 feet since starting our journey down in the valley far below, making our ascent equivalent to trekking some 1,300 miles north to the Canadian Arctic.

Naturally, I'm not thinking about any of this. I'm thinking about how easy it would be to get lost, turned around, and wander off forever into the storm, never to be seen again. Not only do we have virtual whiteout conditions, but of course my goggles are fogging up and the lenses are glazing over. By tilting my head back I can peer through a small patch of clear lens that hasn't yet iced up. With this view, I can vaguely make out the murky shapes of rocks and boulders and place my feet safely, one at a time. Oddly enough, the pummeling wind helps me to navigate these vertiginous conditions. Because the gale is blowing out of the west it is slamming my right side with body-blows, keeping me on a southerly course, steady as she goes.

I almost walk smack into a big rock. Stopping, I tilt my head back and discover that it isn't a rock, it's Joe Lentini.

"Oh, hi Joe!" I shout to be heard over the wind. "I thought you were a rock!"

I raise my goggles to get a better look at him. Mountain guide extraordinaire, long-time leader of the North Conway search and rescue team, and veteran of Himalayan ascents, he appears to be enjoying himself. With a devilish grin and eyes flashing through the amber lenses of his goggles, he leans over against the wind and screams in my ear, "You know, it's crazy, but I love this stuff!"

Mark Twain once said about New England's weather, "If you don't like it, wait five minutes." When we started this traverse two days ago, freezing rain was falling in the valleys. As we began the ascent the conditions turned to lightning and hail. A short time later the temperature plunged and heavy snow began to

Voices in the Forest

Wilderness—not everyone appreciates it, but it is healthy to be where man is not the measure of all things. It's where I feel most theologically at home, closest to real internal insights, to who I am. It's also just very important to have places where life goes on as it always has when you live in a culture that changes as quickly as ours does. We need to be grounded. We also need to be humble in the face of a landscape where we aren't always in charge.

BILL MCKIBBEN, *former staff writer for the* New Yorker *and author of* The End of Nature *and* Maybe One.

fall. South of the mountains and in the region's cities, the winter has once again been marked by wild temperature fluctuations. But up here in the mountains we have a full-blown blizzard. If winter has a home, it is right here. This is where winter lives.

I flash back to yesterday, the six of us huddled among the boulders on the shoulder of Mount Adams like soldiers in a foxhole, with chunks of ice and snow whizzing past us as if shot from cannons. Yesterday was different. It was clear, twenty below zero, and with sixty-mile-per-hour winds gusting even higher. Yesterday, in our relatively sheltered position, we could lean into the wind with all our weight and it would hold us up. But looking off toward Mount Jefferson and Mount Clay, we could see things were different over there. There the wind was shrieking across the Ridge of the Caps, driving before it an enormous billowing cloud of snow rising hundreds of feet into the air. It was terrifying to look at. It seemed nothing human could survive out there.

Not everyone does survive the Presidential Range. Although most of the thousands who climb and ski here every year experience no problems, many people seriously underestimate these peaks, probably because of their modest height. But any misstep or miscalculation up here could be your last. Since 1849, when a young Englishman named Frederick Strickland lost his way in an October storm and perished, the mountain has claimed some 130 lives.

As Joe and I crouch behind a boulder on the ridge, waiting for the others to emerge from the chaos, I reflect on how surprisingly warm and comfortable I feel despite the weather. With the proper layers and shell garments well-matched to the environmental conditions, I have managed to maintain my equatorial temperature despite the mountain's polar efforts to rob me of my precious heat. I feel good about that, but I don't gloat over my success so far. I

Ski mountaineers ascend the fifty-degree slope of a narrow couloir in Tuckerman Ravine on a warm spring day.

can't afford to lose focus or make a mistake. I'm just glad I had the sense to bring the right equipment and go with the right partners.

Like ghostly apparitions, four otherworldly figures take shape out of the storm. Together again, we hold a conference in the lee of the big rock and decide to get off this big rock pile and duck down into the cozy confines of Tuckerman Ravine. Picking out the safest route, Joe leads us through waist-deep drifts down the east side of the ridge to tree line a thousand feet below.

As darkness gathers into an inky night, we pitch the tents by the light of our headlamps. Snowflakes drift through the beams, mesmerizing us in our exhausted state. But it feels great to be so physically tired, to finally sit down and eat a warm meal, to speak without shouting against the wind. Down here in the ravine all is quiet and peaceful, but already I miss the excitement and intensity of the high peaks.

"Hey," says Joe between mouthfuls of some freeze-dried delicacy, "I'm leading a summit attempt on Saturday. Want to come along?"

Head back up there? I think. Back up into the blizzard? After days of being buffeted by storms, I find that I am subconsciously still leaning into the wind. I straighten up, put down my steaming bowl, and consider for a moment.

"Sure, Joe," I say. "I love this stuff!"

BEYOND TUCKERMAN RAVINE

The Gulf of Slides is an extraordinary skiing area. A first reaction on seeing the slides and the snowfield is one of amazement that such terrain can be found in New England. Wide, open bowl skiing and steep alpine runs resemble the Colorado backcountry. There is a wild, untamed feeling about the place.

—DAVID GOODMAN, BACKCOUNTRY SKIING ADVENTURES

Cresting the ridge of teetering, frost-shattered rock, the world falls away at my feet. And when I gaze down into an enormous glacial bowl, I see a wide-open snowfield flow down at an abrupt angle, then pitch over a lip and plunge sharply hundreds of feet to the valley floor where swaths of forest have been obliterated by avalanches. Off to my left, steep couloirs and near vertical snow-stuffed gullies dive down from the mountain rim. To my right, a dozen narrow chutes slash the steep granite face like long white scars.

This is an unexpected, awesome sight. In my mind's eye I see a gargan-

tuan prehistoric cave bear raking and gouging the mountainside with chisel-like claws, sending rock and rubble flying from the heights, excavating this massive chasm called Oakes Gulf high on Mount Washington.

New Hampshire's Presidential Range is truly the peaked roof of New England. Here, the highest summits in the White Mountains soar thousands of feet above treeline and are visible from more than thirty miles out to sea. Grand, rugged, and strikingly alpine, they receive copious amounts of snow. Not surprisingly, the Presidentials have attracted world-class mountaineers, ice climbers, and backcountry skiers for decades. As a proving ground for expeditions into the planet's highest and most dangerous ranges, these peaks have few rivals.

Each spring throngs of adventurous skiers flock to the infamous headwall in Tuckerman Ravine.

Each spring throngs of adventurous skiers flock to Tuckerman Ravine on Mount Washington, some to prove their mettle on the infamous Headwall, others simply to make the pilgrimage to this mecca of American skiing. "Tucks" boasts some of the steepest backcountry runs in the United States, and this is the place where skiing legends have been made since the 1920s. On a warm spring weekend a couple of thousand people will fill the enormous glacial bowl.

The spring trek to Tuckerman Ravine is a ritual skiers have enjoyed for some seventy years, ever since AMC Hutmaster Joe Dodge and his friends made the first descent of the bowl in 1926. Back then, Dodge and company had to bushwhack up the Cutler River drainage in order to reach the ravine— an arduous task that kept the number of skiers in Tuckerman to a handful.

Yet word spread quickly about the extraordinary world above treeline, and increasing numbers of hardy backcountry skiers began making the trip. Before long, the U.S. Forest Service built a trail from Pinkham Notch to Hermit Lake to satisfy the growing traffic to the ravine.

As the years passed the Tuckerman legend grew. Daring feats performed in the ravine by colorful characters became enshrined in American skiing history. In the 1930s Tuckerman was the site of three ski races called the "American Inferno." In one unforgettable race, a young Austrian named Toni Matt tucked straight down the headwall, schussed the Sherburne Trail, and arrived at Pinkham Notch in 6:29:2, beating his rival, Dartmouth ski champion Dick Durrance, by a minute.

"Being nineteen with strong legs, and stupid, was the right combination at the right time," said Matt of his victorious run.

Today skiers still make the three-mile-long hike from the Appalachian Mountain Club's Pinkham Notch camp to the base of the ravine to ski or snowboard. But plenty of people also come simply to watch, while still others trek up the mountain in costume to entertain the crowds. Tuckerman is a natural amphitheater, and I once saw a big green fish in concert at "Lunch Rocks," the main hangout for nonskiing revelers. While skiers with white knuckles, weak knees, and sweaty palms contemplated the Lip and the Chute, the fish played the guitar and sang beautifully, delighting the festive crowd. There's simply nothing else like Tuckerman. It's the world's oldest and grandest carnival of skiing, a Mardi Gras celebration of the simple joys of sliding on snow.

But while skiers from around the globe may have heard of Tuckerman,

OPPOSITE:
Mark Heckman telemark skiing the extreme steeps of the Great Gulf. The summit of Mount Washington and the towers of the Mount Washington Observatory rise behind him.

Voices in the Forest

The Green Mountain and White Mountain National Forests are excellent examples of how all the Northern Forest should be operated. They are models for the rest of the country. No other forests must satisfy as many competing interests. And by and large they are doing a damn good job. If all this land were to be included in the national forests, and were managed as well as the White Mountain National Forest is, then I would be very happy. But people's attitudes are slow to change. There is fear that government ownership would lock people out. We just have to make sure that the guy with the lunch pail, the guy driving the skidder, is a part of the picture.

JOHN HARRIGAN, *Coos County, NH, newspaper publisher, sportsman, and columnist.*

few realize that this touchstone of American skiing is but one of many large, glacially carved alpine cirques on Mount Washington and in the rest of the Presidential Range. Ravines such as the Gulf of Slides, Oakes Gulf, and Ammonoosuc Ravine are just as big and steep. To be sure, Tuckerman is the most storied of these bowls as well as being the easiest to get to, but by no means does it offer the only high-quality skiing experience in the range. To access the rest of the terrain you just have to pay the extra price in sweat and aching muscles. It's a cover charge relatively few are willing to shell out.

Up in Oakes Gulf, professional extreme skier and Warren Miller film star John Egan and I have made the investment, making the long hike up to Oakes Gulf together with some friends. We duck behind a boulder below the ridgeline to get out of the wind, which still has a wintry bite to it even in May.

Egan, who has skied all over the world but who chooses to live in Vermont, seems as bewitched by the grand scale of the scene before us as I am. "We could spend days up here, easy," he says. Then he points into the distance with a ski pole. "Look at those steep lines over there across the gulf. There's a lot of great skiing here, this is world class."

Snapping in to my telemark ski bindings, I slide over to the top of the snowfield and watch Jim Bohringer attack the slope. His skis fling waves of soft wet snow left and right as he banks sharp turns down the fall line before disappearing over the lip. There are about fifteen of us here in Oakes Gulf today. But aside from our little gang, the ravine is empty (meanwhile, there are probably a couple of thousand people in Tuckerman).

In the late afternoon we descend the Presidentials via Ammonoosuc Ravine, another majestic chasm with sheer slopes plummeting to the forested valley below. It's as if we have discovered a lost world of rock, ice, and snow concealing some of the most exciting and challenging runs I've ever skied.

A few days after our exploration of Oakes Gulf and Ammonoosuc Ravine, I'm hiking up another rocky trail in the Presidential Range with a group of friends. With skis strapped to packs, and packs strapped to sweaty backs, we clamber over the boulders in our ski boots. When we finally crest the summit ridge, we feel a blessed snow-cooled thermal updraft sweep over us from the depths of the canyon below.

Perfect telemark form on a warm spring day in the Presidential Range.

At the top I enjoy my first hard-won view of the Great Gulf, another of the range's little-known skiing treasures and the largest glacial cirque in the White Mountains. Below me waiting to be skied is the biggest, wildest abyss I have seen in some time. It plunges straight down for more than 1,500 feet and stretches into the distance for more than three and a half miles. To the north the alpine crests of the Presidentials—Mounts Clay, Jefferson, Adams, Madison—march off in a jagged snowcapped line, while to the south the massive summit cone of Mount Washington probes the sky.

Skiing Pipeline Gully in the Great Gulf feels like jumping into an elevator shaft. The narrow tongue of snow plunges between towering rock walls, and the relentless angle never lets up as the couloir plummets toward the sapphire ice of Spaulding Lake far below. Pipeline is one of the cleanest, most aesthetic lines I have ever skied, but it's just one of many here, and we spend the day skiing, climbing, and exploring, getting to know this remote mountain chasm.

Later, back at the trailhead, it strikes me as ironic that by staying home and exploring the nearby wild instead of hopping a plane bound for exotic ranges, my world has expanded. I always knew there was tremendous big-mountain back-country skiing in Tucks, but when I consider the astonishing world I've discovered beyond Tuckerman Ravine in places like Oakes Gulf, the Gulf of Slides, Ammonoosuc Ravine, and now the Great Gulf, I no longer envy boastful Westerners their 10,000-foot peaks. This is as good as it gets.

WHITHER THE
YANKEE FOREST?

THE FOLIAGE ALONG THE WOODS road north of Guilford, Maine, is incendiary. At every bend the mixed northern hardwood forest—that volatile brew of beech, birch, maple, cherry, ash, and aspen peppered with black spruce and fir—detonates into excruciating bursts of red, yellow, and orange brilliance. I catch myself alternately raising and lowering my sunglasses, deciding whether to expose my eyes to the splendor with or without the amber filters. I finally opt for the natural effect—I want the full, rich experience.

Overhead, above the bright palette, is a dark, stormy sky. Beams of sunlight slide beneath the black clouds the way light slips into a gloomy cave entrance. While the immediate foreground is dazzling, the background is brooding, almost theatrically sinister. A wind with the feel of winter shakes my old truck now and then. Scattered showers contradict the golden light. We are alternately warm and cold. The seasons are in transition. It's autumn in the Great North Woods of Maine.

My companions on this fall morning are Martin Leighton, who has worked in these woods for all of his seventy-some years save for a stint fighting in the South Pacific during World War II; and Yankee, Martin's dapper seventeen-year-old pure white Samoyed-Lab mix with jet-black eyes whom Martin always addresses deferentially as "Sir."

"Please get in the truck, Sir."

"Have some water, Sir."

A giant Mack truck is dwarfed by a woodpile in the log yard at a paper mill in Rumford, Maine.

153

As we round a bend in the road the colors vanish. The trees—all of them—have been removed by the landowner, one of the multinational paper companies, in a clear-cut operation. The cut is modest for up here, for I guess it is only about one hundred acres or so, but it is a jarring sight nonetheless. The abrupt contrast with the neighboring forested tracts is unsettling. I have passed this cut a dozen times before, and its location, completeness, and total exposure to passersby are impossible to ignore. The cut is a bald statement, as obvious and deliberate as a roadside billboard. Each time I pass it I can't help but wonder—is this the future of the Yankee forest?

These woods are New England's and upstate New York's great treasure. From the offshore islands the forest jumps to the mainland and floods north and west. It laps at the crests of the White Mountains and the rugged Katahdin massive, sweeps toward the Saint Lawrence and Saint John Valleys, spills over the spine of the Green Mountains, Berkshires, Taconics, and Adirondacks. Millions and millions of acres of forest, binding the soil, controlling the watersheds, cooling the air and soil, breaking the wind, sheltering the wildlife, nurturing the fisheries, providing homes, recreation, employment, and sustenance to the people of the region.

For over a century, Millinocket, Maine, has been a leading center for the production of pulp and paper.

The Northeast is the most heavily forested part of the country, and Maine is our most heavily forested state. I once read somewhere that if all of New England's forests were cut down at once, and the wood were stacked in cords—four by four by eight feet—the resulting woodpile would circle the globe at the equator some forty times.

To be a Yankee has always meant to live among trees. To work in the woods, to "let daylight into the swamps" as the old-time woodchoppers used to say, is one of our oldest and proudest occupations. To recreate in the woods is one of our timeless pleasures. The Yankee forest has always been our great wealth and comfort.

So it is little wonder that the sight of a clear-cut is unsettling to many New Englanders and upstate New Yorkers, no matter how valid the commercial or silvicultural reason. For many Yankees, the wholesale removal of our forests feels like the betrayal of a sacred trust.

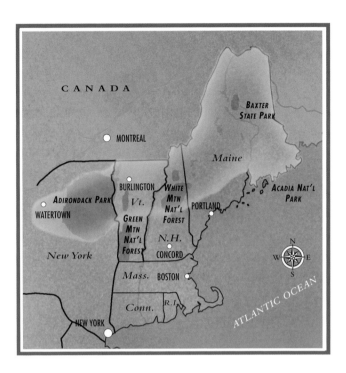

"Please get out, Sir. We're going for a walk."

Martin, Yankee, and I leave the truck parked on the shoulder and walk out into the clear-cut. Beads of moisture on the leaves of emerging pin cherry, aspen, raspberry, and other pioneer species catch the sunlight. The walking is difficult over the stumps and slash—piles of broken branches, bark, and woody debris left behind by the harvesting machines—and we take our time. After about fifty yards we stop and look around. We let the feel of this new landscape settle.

More than half a century ago, when Martin first started working in the woods, operations like this were unheard of.

"In the mid-thirties, by the time I was twelve and really traveling the woods, there were big trees, old growth, wherever we went," says Martin. "Everyone worked the woods, but they didn't hurt the woods. There were cuttings, but they didn't cut hard. If the woods had been clear-cut, it would have been gone when I went into it as a kid."

We look at the remains of the forest around us. The stumps are tiny—barely seven to ten inches in diameter at the base—Lilliputian compared to the forests Martin remembers haunting as a young man. Those forests were stocked with trees that went twenty to thirty inches in diameter and more, sometimes much more.

"I came into the woods at the end of an era," he continues. "Back then, Maine woodsmen were farmers, mostly. They did their farming in the summer, and cut wood in the winter. They put their horses to work year-round. You can visualize how many people were employed. Our town was a little bigger then than it is now, and everyone worked, everyone made a living."

OVERLEAF:
The clear-cut is a bald statement, as obvious and deliberate as a billboard. Is this the future of the Yankee Forest?

In the Northern Forest, the woodchopper and river driver was every bit as romantic a figure as the cowboy was out West. The men who worked in the woods in the first decades of the 1900s were a polyglot mix of Yankees, French Canadians, and Indians, along with a smattering of Irishmen, Swedes, Finns, and Poles. They were expert at timber felling, boat handling, dam building, and saloon fighting. Their job was dangerous, physically demanding, and required highly honed special skills and sharp reflexes. The work took place away from the restraints of civilization, deep in the winter woods at thirty below zero and in the icy rushing rivers and streams in the spring.

They were proud men, and tough. Far from medical assistance, they treated cuts with chewing tobacco then sewed them up with needle and thread. They drank spoonfuls of kerosene to settle upset stomachs. And when

the drive was done they weren't averse to stomping an opponent with their spiked boots in a bar fight—many a woodchopper's face bore the ravages of "logger's smallpox." To be a woodsman—felling the giant trees by hand, riding the long logs as they careened down swollen waterways—took tremendous courage, strength, and know-how. Despite the physical hardships, the miserable living conditions, and the low pay, it was an exhilarating life, and it made ordinary jobs seem dreary by comparison. As one-time New England woodsman and historian Stewart H. Holbrook recollected in *Yankee Loggers:*

> Few of us boys wanted to be soldiers or cowboys or policemen. To be a
> riverman and go down with the drive was the stated or secret ambition
> of most of us. To ride a heaving log through white water, to steer a bateau

*Martin
Leighton and
his dog, Yankee.*

down Fifteen-mile Falls, to break a jam anywhere—these were the most important things one could hope to do. What we wanted, in that time and place, was a cant dog, a pair of new calked boots, and a fast moving stream of logs.

And the world of the Yankee forest Holbrook yearned to enter as a boy was truly a magic realm, a place apart:

For us logging camps had all the magic of the Land of Oz. (It was not until later that we came to appreciate the great ingenuity of the woodsmen who not only built the camps, but all their furniture and fittings, too.) Half-savage places remote from town, yet alive with shouts and the sound of bells and creaking runners, they seemed like stars in the vast forest night and mystery of spruce and fir and hemlock. The forest was dark enough, but never quiet for long. At night it snapped and crackled and boomed from bitter cold. By day it echoed from ax and saw, with only a momentary pause when a felling wedge went home and a big, tall spruce came swishing down to deep silence in the snow.

In 1900 some 30,000 men worked in the Maine woods seasonally. By 1970 logging was no longer a seasonal activity, and just 6,500 men logged full time. By 1988, there were a mere 3,660 men working in the woods full time—a third of them Canadians. And yet ironically, concurrent with the dramatic job losses, the total wood harvest in Maine doubled from 1940 to 1970, and doubled again by the mid-1980s.

OPPOSITE:

*A classic
"beauty strip"
hides a clearcut
in the Maine
woods from the
view of any
passing
canoeists.*

When Martin began working in the woods in the years before World War II, he and his fellow loggers worked through the winter, using bucksaws and axes to fell the tall trees. They yarded the logs with horses—"twitched 'em to the hot yards in the woods"—says Martin in his classic Downeast brogue—"then two-sledded the logs with horses over the slick tote roads and stacked 'em on the ice of the big lakes." When the ice went out in the spring the men floated the logs down the frigid streams to the mills. It was tough, dangerous

work, extremely labor intensive, but it provided needed seasonal employment for the local farmboys.

There was another benefit to the labor-intensive, seasonal logging that Martin knew as a young man: it was easier on the forest. Deep snow protected the young growth, selective logging techniques preserved the integrity of the forest, and the tools of the trade—axes, bucksaws, horses, sleds—had much less of an impact on the environment than today's modern equipment.

After World War II, the chain saw replaced the ax and bucksaw, and by the 1960s the mechanical log skidder replaced the horse. Meanwhile, the diesel semitruck and the woods road replaced the river drive. By the early 1960s there were some two thousand miles of woods roads in the forests of northern New England. Now there are an estimated twenty thousand miles of woods roads in the state of Maine alone. Whereas only forty years ago it was possible to cover huge roadless tracts by snowshoe or canoe, it is virtually impossible to put more than five miles between yourself and a road anywhere in the Maine woods today.

> ## Voices in the Forest
>
> *We haven't shown the will to educate ourselves and solve our problems. I used to think there were solutions, but the older I get, the more I doubt it. We all have too much self-interest. And we are a species out of control with our birth rate. Nature will take its course. She will find the solution to all our problems. And yes, there will be suffering.*
>
> STEVE MONGAN, *forester for Landvest.*

Chain saws, skidders, and roads had huge impacts on the woods and on the work force—with each innovation more wood was cut by fewer people, and the roads diminished the wildness of the region by rendering even the most remote areas accessible by car. But it can be argued that the mechanical harvesting machine—the fellerbuncher—has had the greatest impact of all on the Yankee forest.

OPPOSITE:

Softwood trees in the grasp of a mechanical harvesting machine, or "fellerbuncher," near the West Branch of the Penobscot River in Maine.

Each fellerbuncher does the work of up to a dozen men, cutting up to a thousand trees per day. They are terribly efficient, but because of their great size they are anything but discerning. These giant machines cannot possibly slip between trees to selectively harvest a stand—they must take the whole forest down. And because they are so expensive, costing hundreds of thousands of dollars, their owners cannot afford to keep them idle. Consequently, the machines run eighteen hours per day, all year long, except in early spring when the ground is too soft.

The clear-cut Martin, Yankee, and I examine is the work of one of these

machines. Every tree stem has been snipped, the ground is rough and uneven from the passage of the behemoth. On the way back to the truck Martin tells me about watching a man operating a fellerbuncher.

"For every one hundred cords of merchantable timber he cut he was just trashing another hundred cords because it wasn't worth it to him to be careful," he says.

Gone now are the colorful characters that once went to the woods, ax in hand, to fell the big trees. The walking bosses, the choppers, the river pigs, and the bull cooks are seen no more in the Northern Forest, and the woods seem diminished. Gone too is the rich culture of the log-driving era, including the vivid language the woodsmen once used. Theirs was a verbal mulligan stew, a private argot filled with words such as "birling," "short-staker," "swamper," "wanigan," and "peavey." To the bafflement of outsiders, they scattered their sentences with references to the "sky hook," the "cross-haul," the "deacon seat," and the "sprinkler sled."

Having the skills and knowing the arcane language meant membership in a special club. And when the woodsmen came to town at the end of the drive flush with pay and pent-up appetites, they were treated like conquering heroes. Like cowboys "painting the town red," the logger's lusty sprees were the stuff of legend. But when the machines took over, working in what came to be known as the "forest products industry" became just another low-paid tedious job, the woodsman became just another laborer, and the profession lost its mythic status.

At the same time the steel behemoths began replacing the men, they began wreaking havoc with the environment. Critics now accuse the fellerbunchers with crushing forest undergrowth, damaging uncut trees, destroying young seedlings, compacting the soil, causing erosion, silting trout and salmon streams, and increasing the trend toward larger and larger clear-cuts.

An hour later, driving along a woods road not far from the West Branch of the Penobscot River, Martin and I see just what the forest products industry is capable of. Here, in relatively flat spruce-fir country, we use the truck's odometer to clock what the industry calls a "rolling clear-cut."

Heading south to north, we traverse the giant cut for a little more than eight miles. We know from a previous trip that the cut also extends east and west for a similar distance, making this one cut roughly sixty square miles. The big machines have stripped the land bare. As we drive along I tell Martin what Chief Homer St. Francis of the Abenaki told me one day in Swanton, Vermont: "They are vacuuming the forest," he said. "You can write down how there used to be a forest. Now we are looking for the rest of it. They don't leave a goddamned thing."

Unlike harvested areas of earlier times, this cut has been sprayed with poisonous herbicides to eliminate the regeneration of shrubs and hardwoods that naturally colonize open areas. In place of these natural pioneer species, the landowner has replanted a softwood monoculture. By so doing the company is encouraging the growth of the more commercially viable species which is used for paper while eliminating the rich natural biological diversity of the site.

The cut-over, sprayed, and replanted land rolls on to the horizon. In some places the planted spruce appear to be doing well. In others, there doesn't appear to be any new growth at all. Martin shakes his head.

"Damn it," he growls, "some of this land was meant to grow hardwood. They're changing hardwood land to softwood. It's not natural, and it just isn't working, obviously."

"I don't foresee this land ever growing back to real wood," he says. He is referring to the bleak landscape beyond the cracked and pitted windshield, but I sense he is really talking about the Yankee forest as a whole. "It's all just chip wood," he continues. "So much of the large, healthy wood has been cut in the last thirty years. I tell you this crop of planted wood will never replace the forest I knew as a child.

"And these clear-cuts are drying right out," he says, waving a gnarled hand out the window. "I've seen places where the aerial poison spraying has killed the very earth itself. But I'll tell you this—no matter how bad things have gotten, worse is yet to come," he assures me.

"You know," he says after a mile or so, "these woods would grow back if we just allowed it. But nature can't overcome what we are going to do to it to satisfy our insatiable demands. It's what's going to be done from this moment forward, not even what has been done till now, that will spell the end of the woods. There is just no way to stop it. There simply aren't enough resources to support our ever growing human population."

We exit the giant clear-cut and enter a different corporate ownership. Here are trees again, bright and colorful in their autumn hues but still not quite

> ## Voices in the Forest
>
> *I'll give you the Abenaki perspective on the Northern Forest. When I'm over in Island Pond, over in Canaan, when I drive through the forest, I see the trees that were there. It reminds me of where the Abenaki people are—struggling, but still here.*
>
> THOMAS OBOMSAWAIN, *Abenaki Ambassador, Swanton, Vermont.*

a healthy looking forest. The trees are small, stunted, as though the best stock had been removed and a forest of runts left behind. Later, my suspicions are confirmed when the author of a book on modern forest management tells me that these particular woods are a classic example of "high-grading," meaning that the most valuable timber is logged, leaving behind the weaklings and depleting the forest's gene pool.

On the drive back to Guilford, Martin and I discuss both the glorious past and the uncertain future of the Yankee forest. We talk about the log drives that took place each spring from the Raquette River in the Adirondacks to the St. Croix River on the New Brunswick line. Martin reminisces about the "best damned woodsmen in the world," the Bangor Tigers, the Penobscot River choppers and drivers who cut their way from New England, through the Great Lakes, and all the way to the Pacific Northwest. And Martin tells me about legendary characters, men like "Jigger" Johnson, boss of the longest drive of them all—down the Connecticut River from Third Lake on the Quebec border all the way to the booms at Mount Tom in Holyoke, Massachusetts.

Of course, there were plenty of problems in the Yankee forest prior to the advent of the woods road and the fellerbuncher. Disastrous fires frequently burned unchecked across the Great North Woods—800,000 acres in the Adirondacks went up in smoke in 1903 alone. And to the turn-of-the century timber barons, conservation was a heretical notion. They practiced what has generally come to be known as "cut-and-run" timber harvesting. Modern forest science, with its emphasis on sustained yield and overall forest health, didn't really come into widespread acceptance until after World War I.

We stop the truck to let Yankee stretch his legs. While the old gent makes his rounds, I bring up some of the problems in the Yankee forest today. Critics accuse the companies of abandoning sustained yield management and of returning to days of cut-and-run. Mills that have been operating for more than a century are now going bankrupt. Unemployment in the mill towns is reaching staggering proportions due to a lack of a diversity of employment

Voices in the Forest

When I was a kid they cut hundreds of cords of hardwood and never left a hole in the woods. In the fall you had the rock maple, and birch, and beech, and now this contractor goes up there and strips it. Now you can see bare ledge. All the soil's been washed away. When I worked in the woods we cut woodlots that needed cutting, working with horses in the winter. No ruts, we didn't wash the land away like they do now. We only took out some of the big trees and left the rest. 🌰

MERLE WYMAN, *retired logger and farmer from northern Maine.*

OPPOSITE:
An aerial view of a recently harvested area in the Maine Woods. The logs are stacked by the roadside in "landing areas." The next step will be to load them onto trucks that will haul them to the mill.

options. The heavy machines are causing erosion, siltation, and soil compaction. And overall, the heavy industrialization of the forest has reduced the wildlands where larger-than-life figures once trod to mere row crops. The current problems seem overwhelming.

I mention that after his 1853 canoe expedition here, Henry David Thoreau had one of his visionary moments. Two decades before the world's first national park, Yellowstone, was created, Thoreau had the radical idea of creating a wilderness refuge right here in the Great North Woods of Maine. In *The Maine Woods,* Henry wrote: "Why should not we . . . have our national preserves . . . in which the bear and panther, and some even of the hunter race, may still exist, and not be 'civilized off the face of the earth.'. . ."

I suggest to Martin that perhaps Thoreau's crazy 150-year-old idea may still be the best answer, that the only solution to the thorny issues here is the creation of state or federally managed forests, parks, and wildlife refuges. I wonder how an old-time logger like Martin will react to the idea of public ownership, and am surprised when he agrees with Thoreau. He says that he now believes it's the only viable long-term solution, but that it probably won't happen anytime soon.

"So what's going to happen to the Yankee forest?" I ask.

"You'll see a time, probably not too far off, when there isn't a paper company left in Maine," he says. "The kind of forestry they practice here simply can't continue. There will be nothing left to cut! And yet there are *millions and millions more people inhabiting this planet every year*, and the demand for wood products just keeps growing and growing."

"You know," he says, "any solution will have to do with individual solutions. We've all got to change our ways. We can't keep on adding billions of people and expect the planet to keep supporting us. We each have to get our individual houses in order. Then we can demand that these woods be taken care of properly. It's up to each of us to take responsibility, to decide just what kind of a world we want to live in."

We lean against the truck and let that thought sink in for a few moments. And then Martin says, "Alright, Sir. It's time to go home."

On the long drive back to Guilford the three of us watch the ravaged woodlands pass by the dusty windows. Ahead, through the pitted windshield, the setting sun strikes Katahdin's knife-edge, making it pulse and glow like hot forged steel. A shadowy moose-figure crosses the road a hundred yards in front of us, and Yankee watches it intently with obsidian eyes. Suddenly it occurs to me that we haven't seen another person all day.

And then I realize why I haven't given up on this place. For one thing, torn and tattered though it seems, it's still here. It hasn't yet been turned into subdivisions. In recent years the people of the region have banded together and begun using an assortment of creative conservation tools to protect hundreds of thousands of acres. Today, much of the Yankee forest is still a vast unpeopled and undeveloped landscape—in some ways, it's a frontier, a place whose future can still be determined. As the old truck shudders over the washboards in the falling dark, I have an odd feeling, a small swell of hope. It could happen. Maybe everything these woods once were, and everything they once supported, can be restored.

EPILOGUE

NﻟORTH OF PITTSBURG, NEW HAMPSHIRE, we turned off the narrow, frost-heaved ribbon of pavement onto a little logging road. Dan Berns and I were heading toward a network of ponds and beaver sloughs in the forest up near the Quebec border. As I shifted into four-wheel-drive, I glanced out the window and it once again struck me why this area has remained wild for centuries: it was barely late October and there were already several inches of fresh snow on the ground. This part of the country enjoys fewer sunny days than Washington's soggy Olympic Peninsula—and its climate is more like south-central Alaska.

We ran out of road and time at the dark water's edge. Ice was forming in the coves. I shut off the engine and we sat in the silence for a few moments, staring out at the white snow streaking past the windshield.

"This Northern Forest of yours is a helluva place, you know that?" Dan remarked as he opened the door and stepped out. Whirling snowflakes swirled into the cab. "I don't know why I go on these trips with you," he continued as we lifted the canoe off the rack. "I feel like a character in a Jack London story. Last year's snow just melted a week ago. What happened to spring, summer, and fall?"

As we launched the canoe and paddled away, the snow slanted in from the north, driven by a stiff, icy wind that seared my cheeks. Snowflakes stung my eyes. I had to squint to see. If anything, the storm seemed to be intensifying.

I had planned this journey because I believe that to understand a place, to get to know it intimately, requires spending as much time in it as possible. It is hard to get a feel for a landscape—for the sting of wind-whipped fall snow, for the sound of the gale screaming through pine and spruce boughs—without

Silvery branches coated with the season's first snow reach toward a flawless sky, White Mountains, New Hampshire.

experiencing it firsthand. While not everyone can get to these remote areas and learn about them in a direct, personal way, my hope is that this book will bring the landscape to those who cannot make the journey, and perhaps these words and images will inspire them to care about what happens up here.

In this portion of New Hampshire, winter descends with stunning ferocity. From late October or early November, often until well into May, pewter-colored skies spit snow day after day, week after week. For more than half the year these boggy wetlands, tangled forests, and gnarled ridges lie entombed beneath the thick snowpack, while the brutal arctic winds and the bone-cracking cold wreak havoc with everything exposed above the white surface.

The fearsome climate is largely responsible for the ecological character of this region, which bears more resemblance to the Far North than to the more temperate landscapes south of the White Mountains. Extensive spruce and fir woodlands cover the poorly drained, rocky, and acidic soils. Some people, having taken a wrong turn no doubt, pass through here on their way somewhere else and are unable to see this land as anything but useless empty space. But these cold northern forests, rivers, and bogs are a natural treasure chest. They support outstanding fisheries and provide habitat for creatures such as pine marten, lynx, loon, osprey, eagle, spruce grouse, and many, many others.

The climate here sets up strict parameters for human activities as well. Coos County newspaper publisher John Harrigan once told me, "This country is up on the edge. This is where farming came crashing against the woods and petered out. You can literally walk to the last pasture, the last old clearing in the forest, and see where farming gave up."

Up here on the edge where agriculture reached its high-water mark nearly a century ago, logging has long been the economic backbone. Even so, both logging and the human population have been in decline for decades. According to the latest census, fewer people live in Coos County today than at any time since 1940. But those who do live here have learned the skills required to survive in an implacable environment, and along the way have fashioned a tradition of independence that is firmly rooted in this cold northern forest.

Self-reliant and individualistic, the Yankees of this northern land have looked with suspicion upon outsiders and outside authority for centuries. And what was true in the eighteenth and nineteenth centuries still holds true today. The Yankee character views the world askance, and yet to me it seems perfectly understandable for a people with intimate knowledge of their local landscape to look upon outsiders—who have at best a superficial grasp of the complexities of the physical and cultural geography—with wariness.

People's lives up here are largely orchestrated by the rhythms of the seasons. The primary occupations are directly tied to the land, and so are most recreational activities. Whether felling trees, making maple syrup, gathering berries and mushrooms, hunting deer, snowshoeing, canoeing, trout fishing, or snowmobiling, most residents of the Northern Forest engage in a rich pallet of landscape-based seasonal activities.

So in July 2001 when the International Paper Company put all 171,000 acres of its timberlands here up for auction (including eighty percent of Pittsburg, which at 142,458 acres is one of the largest towns by area in the United States, but a metropolis of only 867 people), there was widespread concern that the rugged landscape and the rural way of life it fostered might be lost forever. A private group, the Trust for Public Lands (TPL), immediately stepped in, temporarily saving the land by purchasing it from International Paper. The TPL action gave a task force co-chaired by New Hampshire Governor Jeanne Shaheen (a Democrat) and U.S. Senator Judd Gregg (a Republican) time to seek input from the local people, study the situation, and make suggestions.

The task force's final report recommended purchasing a conservation easement to be owned by the State of New Hampshire covering the entire property, selling timber rights with a timber management plan on 146,500 acres to a private company, and setting aside a natural area owned by the state covering 25,000 acres. Through their swift action, federal, state, and local officials of both parties successfully worked with private conservation and timber organizations to create one of the most signficant conservation easements in American history. In an unprecedented achievement the task force not only protected an irreplaceable landscape, but a traditional way of life as well.

When I heard the news, I remembered how John Harrigan had said that this landscape was "up on the edge." Time to change that to the *cutting* edge, I thought. With the purchase of these lands, the people of the North Country showed us all that the land, the jobs, and the rural way of life are inseparable. To save the one, you have to save them all.

Dan and I camped in the snow that night, just like characters in a Jack London story. We built a fire, but we came to no untimely end. By morning the snow tapered off, and we took advantage of the clearing weather by spending the day reading the fresh white landscape, tracking snowshoe hare and grouse. As we hiked we found the signs left by coyote, deer, porcupine, and pine marten. Later, we found large depressions in the snow where moose had spent the night, and another tight spot where deer had funneled through. Mile after hard mile, the Northland revealed her mysteries to us. We in turn confirmed that this landscape was anything but "good-for-nothing, empty space."

Now, as we paddle back to the put-in on this chilly autumn evening, a ragged skein of Canadas fills the air with goose music. Looking up, I think of all the mostly magnificent, but sometimes depressing, places I have been in the Northern Forest over that last several years. I look back upon the thousands of miles I have traveled by canoe, kayak, dogsled, pick-up truck, float-plane, schooner, ski, snowshoe, and on foot, criss-crossing the region in all seasons of the year. I see again the faces of my many traveling companions and mentors, men and women who have enriched me beyond any reasonable expectation with their insight, knowledge, and experience.

Many of us have a dream for the Northern Forest. My dream is that we will preserve the beauty and the wildness of this great land while protecting respectful human participation in the landscape for generations to come. And as we near the take-out of this last journey, I hope that in some way this book will help fulfill these dreams.

OPPOSITE:
*Day draws
to a close
in the
Northern
Forest.*

1631 The North American lumber industry is born when a water-driven sawmill is built on the Salmon Falls River in South Berwick, Maine.

1734 Lumbermen in Fremont, New Hampshire, illegally cut Mast Trees reserved for the King's Royal Navy. When the Surveyor General, David Dunbar, visits the mill to inspect the fallen timber, he is attacked and chased off by a mob of local citizens disguised as Indians.

1759 From their base at Fort Crown Point, New York, Rogers' Rangers, the precursors of today's Special Forces, attack the Abenaki village of St. Francis, Quebec, deep behind enemy lines, dealing a devastating blow to the French and their Indian allies during the French and Indian War.

1839 Maine declares war on Great Britain over a boundary dispute between New Brunswick and northern Maine, the only time a state has declared war on a foreign power. The conflict known as the Aroostook War is settled before shots are fired.

1847 George Perkins Marsh, a U.S. Congressman from Vermont, delivers a speech to the Agricultural Society of Rutland County, Vermont, calling for a conservationist approach to forest-lands management. In his speech Marsh points out the many destructive impacts of deforestation.

1851 Henry David Thoreau addresses the Concord Lyceum, declaring that "in Wildness is the preservation of the World."

1857 Samuel H. Hammond publishes *Wild Northern Scenes; or, Sporting Adventures with the Rifle and Rod,* one of the earliest volumes in the emerging hunter-conservationist style. The book celebrates the beauty and value of the Adirondack wilderness and promotes the preservation of wilderness areas as places for recreation and spiritual rejuvenation.

1858 Joseph Peavey, a blacksmith in Stillwater, Maine, invents the "cant-dog," or "Peavey," a pole with a hooked end that allowed woodsmen to maneuver fallen logs with relative ease. The tool is still in use today.

1860 Frederic Edwin Church paints his masterpiece "Twilight in the Wilderness," a landscape of Maine. During the mid-nineteenth century he and several other eminent artists of the Hudson River School, including Thomas Cole, Fitz Hugh Lane and Albert Bierstadt, explore and celebrate the power and beauty of the American landscape.

Thomas Starr King publishes *The White Hills: Their Legends, Landscape, and Poetry,* a celebration of New Hampshire's White Mountains in the emerging mid-nineteenth-century tradition of nature-based travel literature.

Bangor, Maine, earns the title "Lumber Capital of the World." In Bangor, 410 sawmills turn out a quarter-billion board feet of lumber annually. The wood is shipped around the globe by some 3,000 sailing vessels.

1862 Henry David Thoreau's *The Maine Woods* is published posthumously.

1864 Vermonter George Perkins Marsh publishes *Man and Nature; or, Physical Geography as Modified by Human Action.* The book is a thorough, ground-breaking analysis of humankind's destructive impact on the environment. A century later, during the heyday of "Environmentalism," the book would be hailed as "the fountainhead of the conservation movement."

1869 A Boston minister, the Reverend William H. H. Murray, publishes *Adventures in the Wilderness; or, Camp-Life in the Adirondacks.* The book extols the beauty of the Adirondacks and advocates wilderness as a resource for recreation as well as personal and spiritual renewal. The book popularizes tourism to the region, but also stimulates public discussion on the necessity of preserving the region permanently.

1876 The Appalachian Mountain Club is founded in Boston, becoming one of the nation's first and most important private conservation organizations. From its outset, the club's mission emphasizes stewardship of the Northeastern wilds.

1892 The New York State Legislature creates the Adirondack Park, including both portions of the Adirondack Forest Preserve and private land holdings, thereby permanently recognizing the region's value as wilderness.

1894 Revision of the New York State Constitution strengthens protection of the Adirondack Forest Preserve by declaring that these lands "shall not be leased, sold or exchanged, or be taken by any corporation, public or private, nor shall the timber thereon be sold, removed, or destroyed." The provision is a victory for "preservationist" conservationists over the "utilitarian" conservationists.

1897 The crosscut saw becomes the tool of choice for felling trees in the Great Northern Forest. This tool allows for two sawyers to do the work of four ax men.

1901 While vacationing in the Adirondack Mountains of New York, Theodore Roosevelt learns he has succeeded to the Presidency of the United States when William McKinley is shot and killed by an assassin.

1911 Congress authorizes the Weeks Act, permitting Federal acquisition of land for the protection of watersheds. The Act also places large amounts of Eastern forest land under Federal jurisdiction for the first time, leading to the creation of the White Mountain and Green Mountain National Forests. After a decade of rallying strong public support for the passage of this act, the Appalachian Mountain Club goes onto play an important role in the development, planning, and stewardship of the White Mountain National Forest.

1915 Despite the opposition of Gifford Pinchot and others in the "utilitarian" wing of the conservation movement, a permanent prohibition on timber cutting in the Adirondack Park is incorporated into the New York State constitution.

The Great Northern Paper Company maintains 1,200 horses in woods camps for hauling logs out of the forest.

1916 President Wilson establishes Sieur de Monts National Monument on Mount Desert Island, Maine, on lands donated by private citizens.

1919 With land donated by wealthy summer visitors, most notably the Rockefellers, Congress establishes Lafayette National Park, Maine, superceding Sieur de Monts National Monument, as the first National Park east of the Mississippi; the park is renamed Acadia National Park in 1929.

1931 Governor Percival Baxter of Maine begins buying the lands around Mount Katahdin that are now protected as Baxter State Park.

1932 Lake Placid, New York, hosts the Olympic Winter Games.

1940 The Connecticut Valley Lumber Company cuts the last large stand of virgin spruce in Vermont.

1955 The gasoline-powered chain saw comes into widespread use in the decade after WWII, replacing the crosscut saw and the ax, further reducing the demand for labor.

1965 The Great Northern Paper Company's horse herd is reduced to only 125 working animals. They have largely been replaced by large rubber-tired, articulated-framed, four-wheel-drive log skidders.

1970 The Allagash Wilderness Waterway is designated as the nation's first state-managed Wild and Scenic River. Under the "wild" designation, the state of Maine agrees to limit road accesses to two or three, prohibit public use of private roads, keep development one quarter of a mile from the riverbank, and restrict the building of any future dams. By 2001, Maine has violated the agreement, allowing the creation of ten public-access roads leading directly to the water's edge.

1975 Woodsmen with chain saws are largely replaced in the Northern Forest by mechanical harvesting machines, or "fellerbunchers" that do the work of a dozen men.

1976 The last log drive in Maine goes down the Kennebec River to the booms in Skowhegan.

1980 Lake Placid, New York hosts the Winter Olympic Games for the second time.

1988 Nearly one million acres of Diamond International Corporation forest lands in the Northern Forest are put up for sale, ushering in an era of instability in the regional forest-based economy and culture.

1990 The United States Forest Service issues the Northern Forest Lands Study, which concludes that "changes in landownership and use clearly threaten the long-term integrity and traditional uses of the land . . . open space, forestry, farming, and recreational uses . . . are gradually giving way to residential and recreational development."

1991 Founding of the Northern Forest Alliance (NFA), a coalition of over forty conservation, recreation, and forestry organizations, including the Appalachian Mountain Club, committed to protecting the 26-million acre Northern Forest. The NFA works to promote sustainable managed timberlands, wildland protection, and strong and economically vital communities.

1994 Authorized by Congress to develop recommendations for preserving the traditional character of the four-state region, the Northern Forest Lands Council releases its "Finding Common Ground" to guide public policy in the region.

1998 An especially volatile period opens as timber companies sell off 6 million acres of forestland in three years, raising new anxieties about development, the loss of recreational access and heavy cutting. With the Northern Forest emerging as a place of national significance, The Conservation Fund purchases 325,000 acres in New Hampshire, Vermont, and New York from Champion International, completing the largest multistate, public-private conservation partnership in history. Soon after, the Nature Conservancy acquires 185,000 acres in Maine's Saint John River valley, in what would be its largest conservation deal ever.

2001 In the world's single largest conservation easement, The New England Forestry Foundation acquires the development rights to 745,000 acres in Maine from the Pingree heirs.

International Paper sells 171,000 acres of land in northern New Hampshire to the Trust for Public Land, who in turn works with other private and public agencies and conservation organizations, including the Appalachian Mountain Club, to permanently protect critical watersheds, important wildlife habitats, and recreational access, and to ensure responsible timber management.

ACKNOWLEDGMENTS

I'D LIKE TO EXPRESS MY GRATITUDE to all who traveled or spent time with me in the field during the creation of this book. The knowledge, insights, and skills you shared were invaluable as I was traveling, researching and photographing this volume. Thanks to Mel Ames, Dick Beamish, Dan Berns, Dee Bright Star, Rob Center, Peter Cole, Alexandra Conover, Garrett Conover, Dave Craxton, John Egan, Rudy Engholm, Jeff Fair, Robert Frank, Annie Getchell, David Getchell, Ed Green, John Harrigan, Kay Henry, Izola Irwin, John Irwin, Roger Irwin, Peter Kavouksorian, Mitch Lansky, John Latterell, Martin Leighton, Joe Lentini, Chris Mangini, Gordon Manuel, Marcia McKeague, Bill McKibben, Steve Mongan, Howard Frank Mosher, Jake Mosher, Dave Mussey, Thomas Obomsawain, Les Otten, Jim Perz, Clarence Petty, Michael Phillips, E. Annie Proulx, Jamie Sayen, Jerry Stelmok, Chief Homer St. Francis, Jym St. Pierre, John Tidd, Brendan Whittaker, Dorothy Whittaker, Steve Whyte, Tom Wildman, Merle Wyman, Yankee, and Greg Zutz.

I am indebted to a wealth of friends and family members for their support and encouragement. Thanks go to Margaret Gorman, David Gorman, Elizabeth Gorman, Mark Kritzman, Ann Borah, Robert Borah, Martha Austin, Ted Austin, Robert Garneau, Susan Garneau, Blythe Brown, Dan Brown, Alexandra von Wichman, Brad von Wichman, Kjersti von Wichman, Peggy von Wichman, Linda Bassett, John "Bull" Durham, Rich Rayhill, Tracy "Grace" Zietlow, Jamie Corsiglia, Richard Drake, Jim Renkert, Steve Vogeler, Rob Durnell, Alex "Alpha Delta" Davis, Melissa Paly, David Batchelder, Becky Moore, Marshall Moore, Kristin Fogdall, Caroline Rush, Sarah Ream, Christopher Johnson, Nicholas Johnson, Candace Kessner, David Kessner, and, of course, the Tasmanian Telemarkers.

And thanks also to the creative folks at AMC Books: Beth Krusi, Blake Maher, Laurie O'Reilly, and Belinda Desher skillfully shepherded this book through from concept to creation. Thanks also to Dede Cummings of DCDesign for her wonderful presentation of this material.

Special thanks go to Rick Bass for his thoughtful foreword to this book.

Finally, my deepest gratitude goes to Mary Gorman for her great spirit, enthusiasm, and support; and also to Tasha for being such a fun, tireless traveling companion.